C. S. LEWIS
Speaker & Teacher

C. S. LEWIS

Speaker & Teacher

Edited by Carolyn Keefe

Foreword by Thomas Howard

ZONDERVAN
PUBLISHING HOUSE
OF THE ZONDERVAN CORPORATION | GRAND RAPIDS, MICHIGAN 49506

CONTENTS

ACKNOWLEDGMENTS

The editor gratefully acknowledges the publishers who have given permission to quote from the following sources:

America for 'Fine Theological Pedagogy' (review) by Harold C. Gardiner.

The Bobbs-Merrill Company, Inc. for *On Christian Doctrine* by Saint Augustine, translated by D. W. Robertson, Jr.

The Bodley Head for *That Hideous Strength* by C. S. Lewis.

British Broadcasting Corporation Publications for *BBC Handbook 1955*.

The Clarendon Press for *The Allegory of Love: A Study in Medieval Tradition* by C. S. Lewis.

William Collins Sons & Co. Ltd. for *They Asked for a Paper: Papers and Addresses, Surprised by Joy: the Shape of My Early Life, Beyond Personality: The Christian Idea of God, Christian Behaviour, Mere Christianity, Miracles, The Abolition of Man, The Case for Christianity, The Silver Chair* by C. S. Lewis; and *The Letters of C. S. Lewis* edited by W. H. Lewis, *Light on C. S. Lewis* edited by Jocelyn Gibb and *The New Testament in Modern English* by J. B. Phillips.

Commonweal for 'Beyond Personality' (review) by Anne Fremantle.

Coventry Evening Telegraph for 'Meditation in a Toolshed' by C. S. Lewis.

Decision for 'Heaven, Earth, and Outer Space', an interview with C. S. Lewis conducted by Sherwood E. Wirt.

William B. Eerdmans Publishing Company for *Essays Presented to Charles Williams* edited by C. S. Lewis.

Harvard University Press for *Philosophy in a New Key* by Susanne Langer.

The Homiletic and Pastoral Review for 'C. S. Lewis as an Apologist' (review) by Thomas A. Fox.

The Macmillan Company for *C. S. Lewis: Apostle to the Skeptics* by Chad Walsh.

The New Republic for 'Mr. Anthony at Oxford' (review) by Alistair Cooke.

Oxford University Press for *The Personal Heresy: A Controversy* by E. M. W. Tillyard and C. S. Lewis.

Princeton University Press for *The Function of Reason* by Alfred North Whitehead.

Faber & Faber Ltd. for *A Grief Observed* by C. S. Lewis.

Sign for 'Beyond Personality' (review) by Philip Ludden.

The Tablet for 'To Mixed Congregations' (review) by Robert Speaight and for 'Clear Reasoning' (review).

Thought for 'Beyond Personality' (review) by John F. Dwyer.

Time for 'Find the Balance'.

FOREWORD

It is a peculiar trait in us all that makes us want to know everything about a great man. If we can find out how Dr. Johnson wanted his eggs, or whether Bismarck wanted the windows open or closed, we will. Data like this may or may not throw light on the man's contribution to the race (literature, politics, science, etc.), but it often seems to. This is why letters and memoirs and biographies catch our fancy: we feel that our appreciation of what the man did will be heightened by whatever we can find out about what he was like.

The more we read about C. S. Lewis, the more it appears that he was a man whose manner, habits, and conversation are not only interesting, but worth knowing about, since they seem to show at work the sort of thing he wrote and spoke about. There is toughness, candour, wit, and imagination in his work, and the people who knew him tell us that these characteristics were visible in the man. He spoke, in one form or another, about goodness and joy and freedom and courage and grief and the fight against evil, and, although he himself would probably have argued that his own *modus vivendi* was of no interest whatever to the public, it is clear that what he said had been not only well thought-out, but tested in experience, most of it very humdrum experience.

My only experience of Lewis other than what I have read by and about him was a brief visit to his house at Headington Quarry a few months before he died. He was exactly what I had expected: he came to the door himself, although he was far from well, in tweed jacket and slippers, and called me by name. His eyes twinkled, and he made some amused remarks about the weather. We sat talking by a small fire for an hour or so. Lewis fiddled with his pipe and smoked one cigarette after another, and I tried to ask him everything about myth and morals and joy and Purgatory and Paradise, plagued all the while with the idea that I was making a terrible job of it and wishing that I had done my home-work better. But never by so much as a cough did Lewis give me to feel that he was anything but wholly engaged by our conversation. I took no notes, although I wanted to preserve every syllable he spoke (I could not bring myself to sit there like a reporter or somebody doing a thesis). My memory for conversations being very bad, I do not remember much of what he said, but various impressions are still lively: there was clarity, agility, merriment, and this toughness and candour which I have mentioned, in the way he said what he had to say. I felt a little like the children in *The Lion, the Witch, and the Wardrobe* felt with Aslan: you knew that gentleness did not suggest weakness. The situation was redolent of terror as well as warmth.

Part of the interest of the chapters in this book on Lewis the speaker derives from the rather personal nature of the studies. That is, most of what is said includes personal observations and experiences of the man, or at least close attention to what he was like, as the backdrop for his work. His ideas are, in a way, *illustrated* for us by reference to the man. Lewis himself, when he was writing and speaking, always found apt analogies and metaphors, since he knew that we are the kind of creatures who grasp things best when they are embodied or pictured. Although he would have waved aside the widespread interest in himself which makes a book like this appealing, he would at least have had to agree that the method is a sound one. And probably, in this one instance alone, the rest of us are better judges than he as to the value of the subject.

THOMAS HOWARD

PREFACE

On the cover was the familiar red border; the picture for the week was a little-known face—serious but pleasant—flanked by a devil and a wing; the name was rapidly becoming famous in the United States: C. S. Lewis.

In *Time*'s cover story written almost twenty-four years ago, C. S. Lewis was acclaimed as 'the most popular lecturer at the University'.[1] A British source also testified to Lewis's ability to attract audiences. Reporting on his death in 1963, *The Times* (London) stated that Lewis and the late Archbishop Temple were the only men who filled the University Church to capacity.[2] Yet in spite of Lewis's recognized effectiveness in public address, not until now has a study of Lewis the speaker ever been published. Several of his talks, however, have appeared in speech and language study collections.[3]

While the discipline of speech has generally overlooked Lewis, English and theology and the publishers have not. A number of doctoral dissertations in English and theology have been written. The published works date back to Chad Walsh's 1949 biography *C. S. Lewis: Apostle to the Skeptics*. Literary critic Charles Moorman includes a consideration of Lewis's writings in his books *Arthurian Triptych* and *The Precincts of Felicity—The Augustinian City of the Oxford Christians*. Roger Lancelyn Green's *C. S. Lewis* and Clyde S. Kilby's *The Christian World of C. S. Lewis* also focus on the ideas found in his writings. Recently William Luther White published a theological exposition, *The Image of Man in C. S. Lewis*. Also in book form are many of Lewis's talks, sermons, and addresses. And scattered through other volumes, primarily in *Light on C. S. Lewis* edited by Jocelyn Gibb, and in dozens of articles and book reviews are comments about Lewis' oral communication.

The writers of the essays in *C. S. Lewis: Speaker and Teacher* have collected some of these comments, searched out new data, drawn from their own experience, and constructed a composite picture of Lewis the speaker. Clyde S. Kilby, Chairman of the Department of English and Literature at Wheaton College, is well-known for his work on Lewis. Besides writing *The Christian World of C. S. Lewis*, Dr. Kilby has produced *A Mind Awake*, an anthology of Lewis's basic ideas, and has edited a volume of Lewis's letters entitled *Letters to an American Lady*. He has been instrumental in securing numerous items for Wheaton College's C. S. Lewis Collection. Stuart Barton Babbage, Executive Vice-President and Professor of Church History, Christianity, and Culture at Gordon-Conwell Theological Seminary, met C. S. Lewis and heard him speak during World War II.

George Bailey, formerly the Executive Editor of *The Reporter* and now a foreign correspondent for *Harper's Magazine*, studied under Lewis at Magdalen College, Oxford University. His chapter is an expanded version of his article on Lewis which appeared in *The Reporter* on 23rd April 1964.[4] Walter Hooper, Assistant Chaplain at Jesus College, Oxford University, served as Lewis's last secretary. Subsequent to Lewis's death, he has compiled a bibliography of his works[5] and has edited several collections of his unpublished manuscripts. Owen Barfield, who says, 'C. S. Lewis was for me, first and foremost, the most absolutely unforgettable friend, the friend with whom I was in close touch for over forty years,'[6] is a retired London solicitor and has been a visiting lecturer in four American colleges and universities. Unlike the other authors, I never met Lewis, but I have heard and analysed his speaking on tape. The last part of the 'On the Air' chapter and the 'Notes on Lewis's Voice' are based on my unpublished master's thesis 'A Case Study of C. S. Lewis's Ten Radio Talks on Love'.

As the editor I extend thanks to those who have contributed significantly to this book. Major W. H. Lewis in personal contacts and in correspondence provided information about his brother. He also granted access to the *Lewis Papers*. Lord Redcliffe-Maud, Master of University College, Oxford, and P. C. Bayley, English tutor, gave permission to quote from the Martlets minute books. Mrs. Caroline Rakestraw, Executive Director of the Episcopal Radio-TV Foundation, Inc., supplied data on Lewis's American broadcasting. Information and help have also been given by Kenneth Adam, former Director of the British Broadcasting Corporation Television; Canon Roy McKay, former Head of Religious Broadcasting of the BBC; the Reverend Joseph Dowell of Wolverhampton; Stephen Schofield, journalist-columnist of Surrey; and Mrs. Joan Ostling, compiler of a comprehensive, annotated bibliography on C. S. Lewis. My gratitude also goes to John S. A. Ensor of Farnham, Surrey for permission to quote from *Answers to Questions on Christianity*; to Stanislaw Jaxa-Debicki, Periodicals Librarian of St. Charles Seminary in Philadelphia, for his gracious assistance; to Dr. Ralph W. Mays of The Germantown Dispensary and Hospital for his medical opinion; to Professor Fritz K. Krueger of West Chester State College School of Music for his analysis of Lewis's voice; and to Drs. Frank E. Gaebelein and Clyde S. Kilby for their helpful suggestions on the manuscript.

C. K.

THE CREATIVE LOGICIAN SPEAKING

CLYDE S. KILBY

Chapter One

THE CREATIVE LOGICIAN SPEAKING

CLYDE S. KILBY

I met C. S. Lewis only once, in 1953. Having some days earlier made an appointment, I mounted the well-worn stairs leading to his rooms at Magdalen College, Oxford, and nervously tapped on his door. He came quickly round his desk and to the door and greeted me warmly, carefully pronouncing my name. Up to that time the only picture I had seen of him showed a vacant stare that was pure rogue's-gallery, so naturally I found him younger and finer looking than I had expected, with a full face, though not fat, and a rather pronounced double chin. The air of good will and utter friendliness about him made me feel immediately at home. He led me around to an old sofa and he himself sat down at his desk, swivelled his chair in my direction, and gave me his complete attention. He spoke as one man to another and without the slightest professionalism or condescension in word or tone.

He was then completing his bibliography of *English Literature in the Sixteenth Century* and laughed about the fact that scholarship is not always as sedentary as is thought. In this case he said he had exhausted himself pulling the great tomes from the Bodleian shelves. I was at the time returning home from two months in Palestine as an amateur archaeologist, and when I happened to mention the fact he was immediately and deeply interested, saying he wished he had had the same opportunity. He spoke of the fact that many writers from the distant past allude to what was for them a distant past. He told of inquiring of a Jewish friend if it were Israel's intention to set up the ancient temple worship and sacrifices in modern Palestine. This man did not know and neither could he explain why the sacrifices had ever stopped. I suggested that I had heard a Jewish lecturer who blamed the cessation on the teaching of St. Paul. Quickly Lewis responded that the Jews had refused to follow Paul and therefore could hardly claim being led astray by him.

All during our conversation he kept working with his pipe, but, if I recall correctly, he never got it really going.

I was then teaching a course in aesthetics and asked him something about the relation of Christianity and art. He promptly responded that it was the same as between Christianity and carpentry. I cited a Christian who claimed that a novel is at best a well-told lie, to which he responded that you are far more likely to find truth in the novel than in the daily newspaper. In fact, he said, newspapers are full of lies and he gave some instances to show their erratic nature when they reported his own speeches. He thought the best evidence of their shallowness is that they never follow up their subjects.

We talked of C. E. M. Joad, professor of philosophy at the University of London who had died a few weeks earlier. Lewis said he and Joad had talked on two different occasions until far into the night and that in the light of these experiences he had changed his mind about him. He had found him sincere—vain but unconscious of his vanity and fundamentally honest in his thinking. He had respect, he said, for Joad's turn to Christianity and was sure he was no charlatan.

My own brief personal experience with Lewis was that of every other American I have heard of who visited him. That is, I found him a man of great courtesy, candour, outgoingness, deep friendliness, quietness of spirit, and manifesting a genuine interest in affairs other than his own. Billy Graham told me of his lengthy visit and of the manner in which Lewis promptly made him feel completely at home.

In later years I once talked with Professor Nevill Coghill at Merton College, Oxford, the long-time friend of Lewis, and he mentioned some similarities between Lewis and the famous Dr. Samuel Johnson. When I incorporated this into a preface I was writing and one of the publishers involved objected to using it, I wrote Professor Coghill of the incident, to which he answered:

I cannot understand how anyone could possibly object to it. There he was, like the Reynolds portraits (bar the wig) thick-set, full-fleshed, deep-voiced, learned, rough, golden-hearted, flattening in dispute, a notable wit, kindly affectioned, with a great circle of friends, some of them men of genius like Tolkien, untidy, virtuous devoted to a wife untimely lost, liable to give his house over to be occupied, or partly occupied, by people less well endowed than himself, dispenser of secret charities, a Tory and a High Churchman. Could anyone since Dr. Johnson be so described except Jack Lewis? And every word true in its fullest sense. When I say 'learned', when I say 'virtuous', I do not mean them in the tomb-stoned sense, where the marble fossilises flattery, but in their most rigorous meanings.[1]

Among other pictures of Lewis, one of the most interesting to me is that of a visit he made to London in 1944 to talk to the Christian Fellowship of the Electric and Musical Institute in Middlesex. Mr. John S. A. Ensor, who arranged the visit, not only allowed me to have his correspondence with Lewis but also wrote me of his own impressions of him. The question arose of the best manner of presentation, and Mr. Ensor suggested simply allowing the men present to ask Lewis questions, to which Lewis replied: 'Now that you mention questions at the meeting it suddenly occurs to me that the best meetings I've ever had have been *all* questions, i.e., I've announced myself as a one-man Brain's Trust on moral and religious questions.'[2]

Someone had wondered whether Lewis's Oxford accent would be understood in London circles, to which Lewis wrote Mr. Ensor:

To anyone who is interested in this vexed question, I wish you'd circulate the *real* answer, which is as follows: 1. The first time I heard my own voice on a

record I didn't recognise it and was shocked. Moral:
A—No man knows what his own accent is like.
B—No man's accent is there because he has chosen it.
C—It may not be the accent he likes. If all my critics
would hear their own voices they'd be very surprised.
2. The whole matter is misunderstood as long as
people insist on looking at accents as subjects of
approval or disapproval. They are simply accidental
phenomena, to be studied as one studies different
varieties of beetles. Taken in *that* way they are very
interesting and often reveal much history. 3. My own
accent is so far from voluntary that I actually *tried* to
retain my original North of Ireland—and apparently
failed. . . . 4. What do they want me to do? I could
try mimicking some other accent but there'd be great
danger, at my age, of producing only a horrible
mixture.[3]

As plans for the meeting matured, the matter of an
honorarium came up, to which Lewis wrote Mr. Ensor:
'I take money for lecturing on subjects on which I'm a
professional (e.g., English Literature), but not for
lecturing on subjects on which I'm an amateur (e.g.,
Theology).'[4] When the time of the visit arrived,
Lewis was to be met at Paddington Station. To help in
identification, he wrote Mr. Ensor: 'I am tall, fat, clean
shaven, don't wear glasses, and shall be in corduroy
trousers, probably with a walking stick.'[5] In later years
Mr. Ensor wrote me:

He did not seem 'fat'. He was dressed in well worn
tweed jacket and corduroy trousers with fawn rain-

coat, and would seem undistinguishable in appearance from scores of other ordinary folk. Looked rather older than expected, although in fact two years younger than I. Had a solitary and detached air, which was deceptive because we almost instantly established an easy and friendly conversation. . . . When we arrived at the E.M.I. Head Office at Hayes, he was taken to a small tea party for refreshment prior to the meeting. Here he met the then President of the Company and several senior executives who had accepted invitations. Although all these men were stylishly dressed and distinguished in their own fields, it was an eye opening experience for me to see the deference with which he was treated in this company.

There were some two hundred present. The Director read the questions. Mr. Ensor reported how 'all the answers were given spontaneously and most eloquently for about one hour non-stop'.[6]

When Lewis made this trip to Middlesex he was forty-five years old and widely known both as an Oxford scholar and professor and a powerful explicator of the Christian faith. In both branches of this rather unusual combination he had published books which won high acclaim.

Now the great and I think all but unique essential in C. S. Lewis's makeup was a remarkable combination of two qualities normally supposed to be opposites. I mean on the one hand a deep and vivid imagination and on the other hand a profoundly analytical mind. Even more remarkable, it was not that these qualities lay in him side by side and disconnected but that by some good alchemy they were organically joined. An easy instance of what I mean is Lewis's *Screwtape Letters* where by the power of imagination the reader is allowed to see his own motives and actions as they are viewed by devils in hell, yet the wide distribution of this book indicates that Lewis put his finger on the pulse of spiritual problems as substantially as any professional theologian could wish. A writer in the *Saturday Review* said that Lewis had 'a powerful, discriminating and, in the proper sense of the word, poetic mind, great learning, startling wit, and overwhelming imagination'. Actually reason and imagination are joined in Lewis's communication—both written and oral—because they were first joined in his thought and life.

The imaginative strain was particularly apparent, as might be expected, in Lewis's childhood. The family's move when he was six to a big new house in Belfast gave him and his older brother Warren a new world of their own. 'I am a product of long corridors', he wrote, of 'empty sunlit rooms, upstairs indoor silences, attics explored in solitude, distant noises of gurgling cisterns and pipes, and the noise of wind under the tiles'.[7] He lived long stretches of unalloyed happiness in his imagination. One cannot forget the nostalgia with which he tells, long after the event, of a time when his brother carried into their nursery a little toy forest which he had made of moss and twigs and flowers on the top of a biscuit lid and of the consequent bliss when, standing one summer's day beside a flowering currant, the memory of that event returned to him 'as if from a depth not of years but of centuries',[8] the two experiences joining to create in him a lifelong love both for the forms and freshness of nature and also the significance of nostalgia, of longing.

In Lewis imagination led early to creativity, and even before he could write, he used to compose stories which he would dictate to his father on Saturday evenings. A little later he was putting other stories down in his own boyish hand. His Animal-Land was patterned on a geography which included India and the Himalayas, and he warned his readers that his stories need not necessarily be taken as history—that they might be 'only legends'. At fifteen he was deeply involved in a project which is almost unbelievable. Preparing for admission to Oxford, he had gone for tutorial study under W. T. Kirkpatrick in Great Bookham, Surrey, and there fallen in love with the countryside and also the glories of Greek literature which he was romping through in the original under Kirkpatrick's tutelage. Earlier he had come to love the whole world of Norse mythology, so now he undertook to write a full-length drama about the Norse gods but built upon a model that was strictly Greek classical. He wrote his boyhood friend Arthur Greeves explaining in detail the contents of Prologos, Parodos, Episode I, Episode II, Episode III, and Exodos, and he urged Arthur, who was talented as a musician, to begin writing the necessary music.[9] Lewis had already begun to write poetry and at twenty published a volume of lyrics called *Spirits in Bondage*.

This imaginative and creative side of Lewis remained

as a major strain and ran like a clear stream in all his oral and written communication throughout his life.

But now I wish to devote a good deal of attention to another and equally significant side of Lewis and one that, as I have said, was seemingly opposite. This side, unlike the other, apparently came rather suddenly into existence when Lewis, at fifteen, went to study under Kirkpatrick. That side was cold-blooded reason. Lewis's own account of how his training began is vivid. The tall, lean, muscular and bearded tutor met him at the railway station and they started for his home. Looking about, the boy began to make conversation, saying that the scenery of Surrey was much wilder than he had expected.

'Stop!' shouted Kirk with a suddenness that made me jump. 'What do you mean by wildness and what grounds had you for not expecting it?'
I replied I don't know what. . . . As answer after answer was torn to shreds it at last dawned upon me that he really wanted to know.[10]

Thus in less than five minutes after they met, Lewis began to feel the sting and forcefulness of a method which he was himself to acquire and exercise for the rest of his life.

The most noteworthy application of the method was that the young atheist Lewis studying under the atheist logician Kirkpatrick eventually discovered that true rationality was the road away from atheism and towards holiness, towards God. Though the road was long—some fifteen years—it became clearer and clearer to the young man who entered Oxford, went away to war, was wounded, re-entered Oxford, was graduated with honours, and settled down as instructor that 'a young Atheist cannot guard his faith too carefully'.[11] God simply closed in on him. The taut rationality and devastating dialectic he had learned from his tutor was largely the means to his salvation. He discovered that a man cannot be intellectually honest with God and fend Him off for long.

The emphasis on reason is everywhere apparent in Lewis's works, fictional as well as expository. In *The Pilgrim's Regress* it is Reason who rescues John from the psychoanalytical prison, slays the Spirit of the Age, offers the prisoners freedom, and leads John back towards the main highway and directs him to Mother Kirk and salvation. Later in the story Reason appears as John's enemy, as he supposes, and forces him with a brandished sword into the right path, the very event which had transpired in Lewis's own experience. In *Screwtape* one of the devil's purposes was to keep the Christian out of arguments about religion. From the hellish point of view was wanted a quiet drift into worldly-wise common sense. Argument would inevitably lead from personal to universal issues, and universals tended to circumvent the insidious schemes of hell.

The most pronounced depiction of the powers and also the shortcomings of rationality appears in *Till We Have Faces*. There the Fox, the Greek tutor of a pagan king's daughters, taught them to reason everything out much as Kirkpatrick had taught Lewis. The Fox explained all the elements of life, physical and metaphysical, as the outworkings of natural and reasonable causes with nothing whatever left over. But later in the novel, the Fox, now in limbo, abjectly confesses that his rationalism had been as clear but also as thin as water. Orual, the leading character in the novel, who had learned her own analytical methods from the Fox, was also dismayed when in limbo she discovered her supposedly airtight case against the supernatural to be little more than a lifelong repetition of a few rather shoddy complaints.

Never does Lewis make fun of reason as an effective instrument, even in the hands of the enemies of Christianity. In *Perelandra*, for instance, Ransom has to confess that at least a portion of the Unman's case is shockingly logical even when in this novel that case threatens to be the cause of a second Fall. It is of course this utter willingness of Lewis to present both sides which has made him a great influence on his generation. In *That Hideous Strength*, Ransom says of his friend MacPhee at St. Anne's, 'He is our sceptic; a very important office.'[12] In the same book, Frost, director of Belbury, explains that much of what one takes for thought is simply a by-product of the blood and nervous tissues and that friendship, fear, resentment, and all social relationships are purely chemical in origin. In what it considered the latest scientific spirit, Belbury set out to treat men as 'machines that have to be worked' and intended ultimately to supplant birth, breeding, and even death with its own particular brand of Rationality.

Against the sterile and decimating technology of Belbury, Lewis in this novel presents two antitheses. One is the re-enthronement of the real 'goddess Reason, the divine clearness' represented by the ancient and worthy, though almost wholly destroyed, strain of true Christianity in Britain. The other is represented by the utter beingness of Mr. Bultitude the bear who did not know that his friends were people or that he was a bear. What he did know supremely was that 'goodness occurred and he tasted it'.[13] Mr. Bultitude lived always in that glorious state of pre-Adamic consciousness that men can only experience in some occasional moment of nostalgia and longing, an experience of 'a potent adjective floating in a nounless void' of pure quality. Like Chesterton, Lewis was a man unutterably appreciative of being itself, such as that in a bear or a blade of grass.

Lewis's conception of reason can, I think, be reduced to two propositions. The first is that of necessity any predication assumes a standard, a norm of some sort, a yardstick. Anything that can be designated thought must be to a greater or less degree involved with the marshalling of ideas into coherent schemes and coercive arguments. An imbecile is what he is because nothing can be error to him. A man can aim his gun at falsehood only when the gun is set against the shoulder of what he, rightly or wrongly, regards as truth. The second is that an adequate standard or norm must rise above the noetic and discursive, that is, reason must give way to a greater thing called Right Reason or, as I have mentioned, the 'divine clearness'.

Both these propositions are illustrated throughout

Lewis's works but are perhaps best illustrated in the three Riddell Memorial Lectures delivered at the University of Durham and later published in his small volume called *The Abolition of Man*. There he begins by citing from a British school book the declaration that when a person calls a waterfall sublime he is making a remark not about the waterfall at all but only about his own feelings. What the authors of this school book are doing, says Lewis, is implanting in the minds of children the idea that all value judgments are subjective and dependent on the accidental factors such as mood or occasion and that there is no more accurate procedure than this. There is really no such thing as a yardstick by which to measure a waterfall or anything else. Such response as one gives is simply relative to the person and the occasion.

Quite contrary to the textbook makers, Lewis holds to what he calls the doctrine of objective value, i.e., 'the belief that certain attitudes are really true, and others really false, to the kind of thing the universe is and the kind of things we are'.[14] He gives this example: it is a fact that children *are* delightful even though he himself does not enjoy the society of small children. When Lewis measures his attitude by the objective value rather than by a psychological response varying according to the mood and the occasion, he is able to recognize it as a defect and to acknowledge that life still demands of him a certain response whether he happens to make it or not. Attitudes, he told his university audience, can be judged reasonable or unreasonable as they conform or fail to conform to Reason.

Even those who go about debunking values practise better than they preach by assuming, often unconsciously, a value of their own. While teaching children that values are subjective and perhaps trivial, the textbook authors are themselves demonstrating that one value is not so, namely, the value assumed by them in the very act of writing such a book. This is apparently a value independent of mood and occasion and is presumably important, else they would not go to the trouble of doing the textbook in the first place. And what is that value actually? That there really are no significant values. Reason thus is used to deny reason and proof is used to prove that proof is chimerical. All arguments denying the validity of thought, says Lewis, 'make a tacit, and illegitimate, exception in favour of the bit of thought you are doing at that moment. It has to be left outside the discussion and simply believed in-in the simple old-fashioned way.'[15] On the contrary, Lewis believes the validity of thought is central and 'all other things have to be fitted in round it as best they can'.

The other idea in *The Abolition of Man* is similar but more subtle. It is the effort, in our time moving forward with dispatch via scientific progress, to reduce all things to 'merely'. For instance, the sun is merely matter, energy, heat, mass, an assumption very far from the belief of the early Greeks that the sun was a god and godlike in its glory. Likewise man is reduced to material —such an object as Susanne Langer describes to illustrate her own complete atheism: man, she says, is 'an organism, his substance is chemical, and what he does, suffers, or knows, is just what this sort of chemical structure may do, suffer, or know. When the structure goes to pieces, it never does, suffers, or knows anything again.'[16] On the contrary, the world for Lewis is not merely factual, nor 'merely' anything, and 'To "see through" all things is the same as not to see'. That is, reason is unworthy of itself until it rises above 'merely'. Abstraction is unavoidable, he feels, but the abstractor must be pertinently aware of the procedure.

In his autobiography, Lewis tells of one of the great intellectual milestones of his education. It arose from reading Samuel Alexander's *Space, Time, and Deity*, where he learned that an experience and the later thought about that experience are two entirely different things that must never be regarded as one. He discovered:

You cannot hope and also think about hoping at the same moment; for in hope we look to hope's object and we interrupt this by (so to speak) turning round to look at the hope itself. Of course the two activities can and do alternate with great rapidity; but they are distinct and incompatible. . . . In introspection we try to look 'inside ourselves' and see what is going on. But nearly everything that was going on a moment before is stopped by the very act of our turning to look at it. Unfortunately this does not mean that introspection finds nothing. On the contrary, it finds precisely what is left behind by the suspension of all our normal activities; and what is left behind is mainly mental images and physical sensations. The great error is to mistake this mere sediment or track or by-product for the activities themselves.[17]

In another place he put the matter very succinctly:

> The more lucidly we think, the more we are cut off: the more deeply we enter into reality, the less we can think. You cannot *study* Pleasure in the moment of the nuptial embrace, nor repentance while repenting. . . . But when else can you really know these things? 'If only my toothache would stop I could write another chapter about Pain.' But once it stops, what do I know about pain?[18]

In *Surprised by Joy* Lewis tells of his pre-Christian excursions, some of them very serious, into philosophies such as those of Bergson, Schopenhauer, Bertrand Russell, Berkeley, Hegel, Occultism, Stoical Monism, Anthroposophism, Realism, and Absolute Idealism. The last was in Lewis's student days the dominant philosophy at Oxford. He came eventually to the conviction that Idealism, taken seriously, was actually 'disguised Theism'.[19] He found that he could incorporate science into his theistic system but that he could never fit Christianity into a scientific cosmology. He wrote:

> Granted that Reason is prior to matter and that the light of that primal Reason illuminates finite minds,

I can understand how men should come, by observation and inference, to know a lot about the universe they live in. If, on the other hand, I swallow the scientific cosmology as a whole, then not only can I not fit in Christianity, but I cannot even fit in science. If minds are wholly dependent on brains, and brains on bio-chemistry, and biochemistry (in the long run) on the meaningless flux of the atoms, I cannot understand how the thought of those minds should have any more significance than the sound of the wind in the trees. . . . I believe in Christianity as I believe that the Sun has risen not only because I see it but because by it I see everything else.[20]

Lewis felt that most of the other popular explanations of things suffer the same inconsistency. Psychoanalysis, for instance, tends to find man 'merely' a bundle of complexes, but we should hardly have psychoanalysis in the first place if the promulgator of that philosophy were himself considered to be simply a bundle of complexes. Again, the Marxist 'proves that all thoughts result from class conditioning—except the thought he is thinking while he says this'. Thus too of Behaviourism, Logical Positivism, or any other philosophy intending explanation by simplicism, reductionism, or naturalistic methods. They are, as G. K. Chesterton said, 'in the clear and well-lit prison of one idea'.

Lewis reminds us of the old problem of scientific explanation itself. If you start out to explain a rose you can ascribe the colour to light waves impinging on optic nerves and scent reaching the nostrils and the like, until no actual rose is left. Such explanations remove us farther from the object we wish to understand. An object does not consist of the elements into which it can be resolved. Like many others, Lewis felt that since the sixteenth century the system of 'truncated thought' at the heart of science has increasingly tended to supplant not only metaphysical and theological thought but true reality itself. He was convinced that reality is more than physical objects on the one hand and abstract concepts on the other; it involves the 'concrete but immaterial' and the possibility of a naked contact with the Almighty Himself.

Now up to this point I have considered mainly the negative side of Lewis's view of reason. If the systems we have mentioned are in error, what is correct?

First, Lewis believed that reason can never properly exist on its own. The plant called reason must have its roots in a deeper soil and its leaves spread out to a more ambient air. Since the human mind is 'wholly incapable of inventing a new value', it must look outward towards a changeless standard. Such a standard is in fact a necessity. 'Our ideas of good,' he says, 'may change, but they cannot change either for the better or worse if there is no absolute and immutable good to which they can approximate or from which they can recede.'[21] One must either accept God as that absolute or inevitably be forced to some lesser, more passing substitute that will become in effect an absolute of man's own making.

When God was, as he says, 'closing in' on him, Lewis was overwhelmed with the idea that God was Reason itself, the very Logic (*Logos*) of the universe. At the same time he was convinced of God as far more than reason, or of reason becoming personal and requiring surrender. He looked back on his long debate with God and discovered that 'When you are arguing against God you are arguing against the very power that makes you able to argue at all.'[22] Up to that time Lewis's non-imaginative universe had been bounded by reason but with some troublesome preternatural elements omitted or else stuffed into a corner. Now he concluded that reason in the normal sense would be for ever insufficient and that something resembling Milton's Right Reason was necessary. He saw with Alfred North Whitehead that, 'Apart from a complete metaphysical understanding of the universe, it is very difficult to understand any proposition clearly and distinctly.'[23] And he also saw with William James that, 'When we see all things in God and refer all things to Him, we read in common matters superior expressions of meaning.'[24] Reason he discovered is the 'spearhead of the Supernatural', but that that reason is conditioned both by Satan's darkening of man's intellect and also by the human condition itself. 'A man's Rational thinking,' he concluded, 'is *just so much* of his share in eternal Reason as the state of his brain allows to become operative: it represents, so to speak, the bargain struck or the frontier fixed between Reason and Nature at that particular point.'[25]

God is not only the source of all facthood but of all order as well, and the source of the moral order. God being absolute and the Creator of all things, 'The real laws of the universe are not broken ever.'[26] Perhaps this is what St. Paul had in mind when he told the Corinthians that 'after all, we can make no progress against the truth; we can only work for the truth.'[27]

After Lewis's conversion he found that Right Reason could easily include in the sum of things not only a Logos or logic but also a personal God of both justice and love. It could accept at once both reason and faith. Faith, he found out, does not consist of tenaciously holding on to a belief without evidence or in the teeth of evidence. A scientist will weigh evidence in a certain way in his laboratory, but he will not use the same process to 'believe' in his wife and children and friends. A Christian believes in God not because he finds Him by laboratory methods but by actual contact with Him. The Christian is something like the electric eel, which knows more about electricity than all electrical engineers put together.

In his communion with God, the Christian moves 'from the logic of speculative thought into what might perhaps be called the logic of personal relations. . . . *Credere Deum esse* turns into *Credere in Deum*. And *Deum* here is this God, the increasingly knowable Lord.'[28] The strict logician versus the believer is illustrated in *That Hideous Strength*. Knowing the menace hanging over them, the rationalistic MacPhee wants to act on the known evidence and finds it impossible to understand Ransom's quiet waiting for orders from a metaphysical world. In a similar way Psyche in *Till We Have Faces* lived inside the glorious reality of her palace and her lover while her sister, the rationalizing Orual, found it utterly impossible to make any sense of the situation.

And now I can return to what I have said of the imaginative and creative side of C. S. Lewis and endeavour to describe the organic joining of that and the rational side.

No longer confined to a God made largely in his own image, Lewis as a Christian discovered a universe increasing simultaneously in wonder and in mystery, a universe more to be celebrated than to be cerebrated. He was like his character Ransom who on the voyage to Mars discovered what he had abstractly called 'space' was now, when he was in the midst of it, a warm and thrilling reality 'tingling with fullness of life for which infinity itself was not one cubic inch too large'. Lewis could now take a new and enlarged look at everything and see cosmic connections everywhere by the use not of reason alone but of Right Reason. He could reexamine mythology and anthropology and conclude, in opposition to Frazer, not that man created God but rather that mythology is the result of 'gleams of celestial strength and beauty' moving upon the minds even of pagan and sinful men. He saw that the world, including its evil, is neither a duality nor an absurdity, but rather the particular sort of world described by St. Paul and Jesus Christ.

Possessor of a God large enough to be inevitably mysterious, Lewis could nose around in all corners and gaze at the magnificent 'oddities' he ran into. There was, for instance, *Sehnsucht*, that longing in every man, that ineluctable cry at the very roots of man's being which keeps man for ever restless until he rests in God. Lewis could welcome the Numinous or built-in awe from man's deep intuition of more than the eye sees and the ear hears. He could try out his friend Charles Williams's co-inherence and substitution and discover that he could actually relieve the intolerable cancer pains in his wife's thigh by taking them into his own.[29] Like Chesterton, he now could readily accept the ineffable richness of the universe and the sensuous world as generous gifts of its Creator. In his poem 'On Being Human' he declares man to be better off than even angels in his ability to feel, smell, taste, hear, and see.[30] Lewis could also fling his imagination forth to depict an unfallen planet and the delightful children's world of the Narnia stories.

Lewis's hierarchy now included God, Right Reason, the Numinous, myth, reality, and joy. He saw the opposite hierarchy as one beginning with agnosticism or atheism and having for its chief members reason, naturalism, scientism, sexuality, such modern jangles as advertising and idiotic sophistication and what Daniel J. Boorstin calls pseudo-events. He saw clearly the subtleties by which the ego falls into the hands of hell.

Lewis's position on reason and Right Reason may perhaps best be summed up by an essay of his called 'Meditation in a Toolshed'.[31] He tells of standing in a darkened toolshed in his yard and seeing through a crack at the top of the door a beam of light from the sun outside. 'From where I stood that beam of light, with the specks of dust floating in it, was the most striking thing in the place. Everything else was almost pitch black. I was seeing the beam, not seeing things by it.' When he moved so that the beam fell on his eyes the whole picture was changed. 'I saw no toolshed, and (above all) no beam. Instead I saw, framed in the irregular cranny at the top of the door, green leaves moving in the branches of a tree outside and beyond that, 90-odd million miles away, the sun.' He concluded that these two views represent two radically different ways of seeing things. Take, for instance, a young man in love with a girl. 'The whole world looks different when he sees her. Her voice reminds him of something he has been trying to remember all his life, and ten minutes casual chat with her is more precious than all the favours that all other women in the world could grant.' But let a scientist come and describe the situation. 'For him it is all an affair of the young man's genes and recognized biological stimulus.' One is looking along the beam, the other simply at it.

Lewis believed that our century has misunderstood Christianity by the illogicality of having not looked along the beam. 'It has been assumed . . . that if you want the true account of religion you must go not to religious people, but to anthropologists, that if you want the true account of sexual love you must go not to lovers, but to psychologists; that if you want to understand some "ideology" . . . you go not to those who live inside it, but to sociologists.' The physiologist may come along and assure us that the mathematician's thoughts are simply minute physical movements of the grey matter in the brain. 'But then what about the cerebral physiologist's own thought at that very moment? A second physiologist, looking at it, could pronounce it also to be only tiny physical movements in the first physiologist's skull.' And so on.

Over against such beliefs, Lewis upholds the power of Right Reason. To be genuinely rational he thinks that 'we must pray for the gift of Faith, for the power to go on believing, not in the teeth of reason, but in the teeth of lust, and terror, and jealousy, and boredom, and indifference, that which reason, authority, or experience, or all three, have once delivered to us for truth'.[32] Only Right Reason is sufficient for these things.

Of course he had no objections to analogical reasoning and in fact, like Plato and others before him, used it freely. A certain theologian thought Lewis's speaking of the Trinity as like a cube of six squares was a vulgarism, but apparently the theologian forgot the vast array of Christ's own metaphors of vines, fig trees, lamps, and bushel baskets to illustrate spiritual truths.[33] Neither had Lewis an objection to anthropomorphic views of God, believing that man has no choice but to make, i.e., to understand, all things in his own image. He often pointed out the fact that seeing God as an old man with a white beard was no whit less anthropomorphic and far more comprehensible than seeing Him as a great Force or Power.

I recall in my youth hearing of Plato and supposing that if I ever tried to read him I should be overwhelmed with the intricacies of philosophical propositions. Then I remember my happy surprise in actually finding in

Plato groups of friends sitting around casually with cups in their hands and talking of packasses and smiths and cobblers and carpenters and beds and tables and magical rings and caves and dogs and birds, and all in a spirit of wit, banter, personal innuendo, and general delight. Always the situation and the conversation were utterly human. Reason is at the bottom of everything, but it is reason lightfooted and joyous, reason filled with anecdote and story. It is as broad as the heavens and at the same time as homespun as a country village.

Such is quite precisely the kind of situation in which I think C. S. Lewis would have found himself at home. In fact, he loved few things better than a group of close friends sitting about a fireplace or out on a vigorous cross-country walk with body at ease and mind receptive to the warm flow of ideas and when everybody was prepared, as his friend Nevill Coghill says, for 'thunderous disagreements and agreements'.[34] Lewis loved the truth but never, if it could be helped, in abstraction. He always preferred the poetic over the prosaic even when he was writing prose. His stories, he said, always began with a picture, not, as one would suppose from remembering his Christian interests, with ideas or 'truths'.

I have mentioned Lewis's appearance before the Christian Fellowship of the Electric and Musical Institute in Middlesex. One of the questions asked him there had to do with the Christian answer to the problem of pain and bereavement. He answered that the best way of response to such experiences is regarding them as proper punishments. 'Imagine,' said he in a figure that would not be unworthy of Plato himself, 'a set of people all living in the same building. Half of them think it is a hotel, the other half think it is a prison. Those who think it is a hotel might regard it as quite intolerable, and those who thought it was a prison might decide that it was really surprisingly comfortable.'[35] Or how could the unique calling of Christ be better depicted than when a little girl in one of his stories wants a drink of water but finds the lion Aslan (Christ) between her and the water.

'Are you not thirsty?' said the Lion.

'I'm *dying* of thirst,' said Jill.

'Then drink,' said the Lion.

'May I—could I—would you mind going away while I do?' said Jill.

The Lion answered this only by a look and a very low growl . . .

'I daren't come and drink,' said Jill.

'Then you will die of thirst,' said the Lion.

'Oh dear!' said Jill, coming another step nearer. 'I suppose I must go and look for another stream then.'

'There is no other stream,' said the Lion.[36]

In such illustrations I believe we find the essential Lewis.

First there is the man of reason and common sense placing before us the simple fact of a thirsty child, a nearby stream and an obstacle. But then the situation is not localized to mere adventure but included the man-to-God and God-to-man framework of Right Reason. And finally the experience is present not as 'statement' but symbol and the symbol is organic to an imaginative encounter between a little girl and a lion.

I have had letters from children or teachers of children, from college students, from businessmen, and from scientists, philosophers, and theologians who have spoken with enthusiasm of C. S. Lewis. The chapters which follow suggest the variety of his talents as lecturer, preacher, teacher, conversationalist, radio broadcaster, and writer. Long ago Lord Bacon said: 'Discretion of speech is more than eloquence; and to speak agreeably to him with whom we deal is more than to speak in good words or in good order.' Lewis knew the art of putting good words in good order and, better still, how to draw close to his audience by cutting a straight path through the mental and spiritual underbrush in which most people are lost most of the time.

TO THE MARTLETS

WALTER HOOPER

Chapter Two

TO THE MARTLETS

WALTER HOOPER

One day during the summer of 1963 C. S. Lewis received a letter from an American university offering him (I believe) £100 if he would pick up his telephone and talk for half an hour on any subject he wished. This 'telephone lecture' would, somehow, be heard by a large audience in the university. To this interesting offer Lewis instructed me to write a 'V.P.R.' (very polite refusal). I was a little disappointed and asked why he refused. 'Because,' he said, 'I can write much better than I can speak.'

This led to a discussion in which I said that, though many of his books gave me the sensation that he was there in the room speaking to me, I had much rather hear his actual voice. 'Don't you think,' he said, 'that many people might be disappointed if they listened to some authors read their own works?' Knowing that he referred to himself, I replied that this was no doubt true of some writers. 'But,' I said, 'I had always rather hear *you*.' Lewis smiled but said nothing. Still wishing to draw him out, I told him that when we first met his accent gave me an unexpected shock. 'But what did you expect?' he asked. I said that before we met I had always 'heard' a soft, Southern American voice speaking, as it were, from the pages of his books.* Lewis roared with laughter and said, among other things, that whereas an Englishman would pronounce both syllables of 'window' very distinctly—'win'dow"—he could remember a Southerner who pronounced it 'win'-duh.'' We grew very merry as we tried to imagine what a Scot, a Canadian, an Australian, and an Irishman would 'hear' when they read his books. (Lewis illustrated the 'low' Belfast accent he sometimes used in Ireland to confuse taxi-drivers who mistook him for an Englishman.)

I went on to say that I believed his readers came far closer than they imagined to 'meeting' him in his books, and that I knew of no author's works in which the human voice and the written word seemed so inseparably combined as in his. 'Perhaps,' he said, 'this is because when I write, I pronounce every word aloud. It's important to please the ear as well as the eye.'

When I first began this chapter, I somehow got it into my head that we could best think about Lewis in two separate ways: as a writer, and as a speaker. I soon knew I was on the wrong track, and I began asking myself how it was that Lewis had learned to bring into such a perfect synthesis the arts of writing and speaking. Judging from his (unpublished) juvenilia, it seems that he had from the beginning an uncommon knack for making his writings approximate the human voice. Nevertheless, I believe his ability to combine writing

* I moved to England from North Carolina.

and speaking was specially perfected by his first experiences at speaking in public. It is these experiences which I have chosen as the subject of my chapter, but I must first digress a little.

Unlike American universities where students receive a large part of their instruction in classrooms, Oxford and Cambridge have what is called the 'tutorial system'. A student who is reading, say, English literature is assigned a tutor who requires him to write at least one essay every week on a set topic. The student goes to his tutor's rooms in college where he reads his essay aloud. The tutor criticizes the essay and gives his student a reading list for help in preparing his next week's essay. There are public lectures which he may attend if he wishes, but the bulk of his work consists in preparing for his weekly tutorials. Whatever else the Oxford student may do with his time, he will have certainly written a good many essays by the time he leaves the university.

When Lewis came up to University College, Oxford, in January, 1919, to read Mods. and Greats (i.e., classics and philosophy), he joined a college society known as the Martlets. Writing to his father about it at the time, he said:

> Much to my surprise I have had greatness thrust upon me. There is a literary club in College called the Martlets, limited to twelve undergraduate members; it is over three hundred years old, and alone of all College Clubs has its minutes preserved in the Bodleian. I have been elected Secretary—the reason being of course that my proposer was afraid

of getting the job himself. And so if I am forgotten of all else, at least a specimen of my handwriting will be preserved to posterity.[1]

The minute books of the Martlets Society are, as Lewis said, lodged in the Bodleian, but I do not know where he got the belief that the Society is 'over three hundred years old': the first meeting is recorded as being held on the 24th October 1892 when a paper on 'The Causes which led to the Renaissance' was read by E. G. Hemmerde.[2] Equally curious is the following inscription found on the flyleaves of volumes II–V of the minute books: ' "The Martlets" Society dates from dim antiquity, but after a temporary disappearance [which lasted only two months], it was constituted in its present form on May 8th 1897, when it was decided that "the efforts of the Society should in the main be devoted to Literature".' What I think quite likely is that 'three hundred years' and 'dim antiquity' both refer to some University College society which in time became officially known as the Martlets. The Society has almost always been limited to twelve under-graduate and former graduate members who hold four meetings each term.

Meetings are usually held in one of the under-graduate member's rooms, each member playing host in turn. For those who are unfamiliar with the colleges of Oxford, it might be helpful if I say a little about what college rooms are like. Though the colleges differ in some ways, it was the practice in Lewis's time, as it is now, for an undergraduate to have two rooms: a large sitting-room which can accommodate about twenty people, and a small bedroom adjoining it. The sitting-room is furnished with a sofa, several armchairs, a table, and bookcases. When a society, such as the Martlets, meets in one of the member's rooms, additional chairs (and coffee cups) are borrowed from a neighbour. The member whose turn it is to read a paper is given one of the more comfortable chairs, and the proceedings begin.

The usual practice in most Oxford societies—literary or otherwise—is for the speaker to *read a paper*. It is, I think I can safely say, as much the expected thing that a speaker will have a paper to read to his audience as that a student will have an essay in his hand when he goes to a tutorial. This was clearly the practice of the Martlets, and, as this book is devoted to Lewis as a speaker, I might mention that I have never heard of him departing from this practice (except in some university lectures when he read from notes) of always addressing an audience with a complete text of his talk before him.

At first the Martlets recorded little more than the titles of the papers read to them and a few caustic comments about some of the members' behaviour. But, regardless of whether they wrote about papers or the more ebullient members of the Society, the Martlets, as Mr. P. C. Bayley observes, 'had always a faint and attractive sense of the absurdity of being self-consciously literary and aesthetic'.[3] I have spent many delicious hours in the Bodleian reading and rereading the five volumes of Martlet history. Before turning to the papers Lewis read to the Society, perhaps I shall be forgiven for recalling a few of my favourite passages.

Two of the founding members I find particularly attractive. The first is Ernest de Selincourt (late Professor of Poetry, Professor of English, Vice-Principal of Birmingham University, and editor of Spenser and Wordsworth) who produced many valuable critical observations. The other is A. L. S. Farquharson who seems to have been singled out for jocular attacks in the minute books. In 1893 'Mr. Farquharson was absent through sheer inertia'.[4] At another time 'Mr. Farquharson was not present for more than 5 minutes in the middle of the meeting'.[5] This lively undergraduate later became the Dean of the College and was for many years a good friend to Lewis. In 1906 he entertained the Society to dinner on the occasion of the one-hundredth meeting. Their literary interests were emphasized in the menu:

> Consommé Mermaid
> Sauce Walter Scott
> Suprême de smale Foweles
> Mouton rôti à la C Lamb
> Chartreuse à la Martlets
> Diablotines à la Milord Byron [6]

There were many members who, if they did not achieve fame, at least contributed to the Society in the way of excitement and entertainment. On the 5th November 1894 the following minute appeared: 'Addison's benefit. Mr. Warwick Draper, who provided the Society with fireworks and rural surroundings, applied the taper with due pomp and circumstance to a set-piece representing his hero in ideal form, with Steele burning in effigy and ignominy behind the scenes.'[7] I find that in the same year 'Mr. Huntington was elected a member of the Society in place of Mr. Campagnac, who has resigned and, like his historical prototype, gone to his own place.'[8] Shortly afterwards 'The Society, on learning of the secession of Mr. Clarke who is discarding English Literature, proceeded to welcome the Prodigal in the person of Mr. Campagnac, who on re-election was at once produced from an Antechamber.'[9]

When it appeared that the minutes were not being kept as carefully as they should be, members complained. At the thirty-sixth meeting in 1900 'The Minutes of the last meeting were read and carried after their scantiness and baldness had been commented on—qualities undesirable in Minutes, which the Secretary strove to excuse on account of the melancholy that had overfallen him as the end of his University career drew nigh.'[10] Occasionally a member had to be jogged out of his indolence. Such seems to have been the case at the fifty-third meeting in 1902: 'It was decided that Mr. Tomlinson should write a paper, or get Mr. Peile to write a paper, or should be expelled from the Martlets. Mr. Tomlinson hummed, hawed, stammered, stuttered, protested, expostulated, cried, screamed, shouted aloud. But the Society was adamant towards Mr. Tomlinson.'[11]

There were social embarrassments when a member

began to probe into improper literary tastes. At the one hundred and thirty-seventh meeting in 1909 the Secretary records:

> For the honour of the Society in the eyes of any who in future years may scan these pages details of Mr. Cecil's paper will not be given. It was not so much Mr. Cecil's inability to cope with his subject: it was not his misdemeanours in point of style: it was the callousness and levity with which he thought fit to treat his paper and call together the Society to hear it. While gravely condemning the lack of application displayed & at the same time accepting Mr. Cecil's unreserved apology, the Society registers its fervent prayer that nothing of the same sort may ever again sully the august pages of its annals. Originality it has always encouraged: but not of this style. If however Mr. Cecil sees fit to apply his disposition for the New in art to an end which this Society can recognize, his well-known talents will be appreciated to full value.[12]

I wonder how many readers would ever guess that the subject of Mr. Cecil's paper was—Robert Louis Stevenson.

Fortunately the practice of the Society when Lewis was an undergraduate was that of keeping very full notes of all their meetings. And, as so few of Lewis's American admirers are able to visit the Bodleian, I feel that I might perform a useful service in quoting at length from the Martlets minute books.

Lewis was elected Secretary upon his joining the Martlets Society on the 31st January 1919. This was the Society's one hundred and eighty-eighth meeting, and the minutes written in Lewis's hand are those for the one hundred and eighty-eighth through the one hundred and ninety-fifth meetings.[13] At the one hundred and ninety-first meeting on the 12th March 1919, while Lewis kept the minutes, a fellow student read Lewis's paper to the Society. It is not surprising that the subject should be one of his favourite authors— William Morris. Lewis must have been too modest to write a full account of his own paper for here is all I find recorded:

After a few facts about the life of Morris and some account of his position in the late romantic movement, he went over his chief works in lyric, narrative and dramatic verse. His early lyrics contained perhaps his most unique contribution to the literature of the period, but 'Jason' & the 'Earthly Paradise' were the works of his maturity and probably destined to enjoy the greater popularity. As a teller of tales he yielded to none except Homer. In his prose works he had endeavoured, with some success, to recall the melody and charm of Malory.

After the interval the usual informal discussion followed. The general sense of the Society was that rather too high a position had been claimed for William Morris. Dr. Carlyle * observed that in his

* The Rev. Dr. A. J. Carlyle, the then Chaplain of University College and one of the best-loved members of the Society.

early lyrical work Morris had probably been writing in a style which was not really natural to him under the influence of Rossetti. Other members commented on the lack of original thought and 'high seriousness' in the poet's work. The Society then adjourned after fixing the place of its next meeting.[14]

Though I find the minutes Lewis wrote very interesting, I think it perhaps unfortunate that he was made Secretary for he nowhere mentions what *he* said in the discussions that followed the meetings. The closest we get to anything like this is a passage about the discussion which followed Mr. C. H. Hartman's paper on Compton Mackenzie at the one hundred and ninety-fifth meeting on the 14th June 1919. Lewis wrote:

The Society thanked Mr. Hartman for his enthusiastic and sympathetic criticism, and after the interval discussed the theory of realism—the discussion soon passing, by paths which the present writer at least has never been able to retrace, into the metaphysical question of 'abstract values'. Mr. Pasley* was adamantine in refusing to allow more than subjective reality to merit in any sphere whatsoever. The meeting then adjourned, after Mr. Watling† had endeavoured to carry a rule that the patrons of the subjective theory should in future be compelled to insert the words TO ME after every adjective they had occasion to use.[15]

* R. M. S. Pasley.   † E. F. Watling.

Added sometime later are the words 'Without success'.

At the beginning of his second year at University College, Lewis was elected President of the Martlets at their one hundred and ninety-sixth meeting on the 15th October 1919. He was prevailed upon to retain this position until he finally insisted upon retiring on the 13th June 1921. While he was President, he read a paper on narrative poetry. An able scribe has given us this lively and full account of the meeting:

The 211th meeting of the Society was held in Mr. Hamilton's ‡ rooms on Wednesday November 3rd 1920. The minutes of the previous meeting having been read and approved, the Secretary informed the Society that an invitation to a joint meeting had been received from the Secretary of the 'Martlets' of Pembroke College, Cambridge. It was unanimously decided that the Secretary should accept this invitation in the name of the Society. The subject of the choice of representatives was then raised, and after some debate the Society agreed to a proposal of Mr. Hamilton that the burden of choice should rest with the President and Secretary. It was decided that the President should, in the event of his being willing, read a paper at the joint-meeting based on the paper which he was to read on that evening.

There being no further private business, the President commenced his paper on narrative poetry.

‡ A. K. Hamilton Jenkin.

He took up, from the first, a fighting attitude. In an age of lyrical activity he was come to defend the epic against the prejudice of contemporaries. Edgar Allen Poe had said that a long poem was impossible, but he was sufficiently answered by the extreme richness of our literature in good narrative poetry. The real objection of the moderns was based on the fact that they would not make the effort to read a long poem. That effort, the reader contended was necessary to the true appreciation of the epic: for art demands co-operation between the artist and his audience. He went on to speak of the poetic 'fullness' of narrative poetry, illustrating the power for tragedy by a quotation from the Tenth Book of Paradise Lost, and mentioning Masefield's Jane in Reynard the Fox as an example of the portrayal of character. Quotations from Spenser showed to what advantage a great artist could use external surroundings as a background to develop a mood. After an interesting digression on the nature and value of 'simile', the President brought his paper to a close. It was as able a vindication of the narrative form as could well be constructed; and it was strengthened by a varied, though certainly not excessive, use of quotation.[16]

By the time he read his next paper to the Martlets, Lewis had taken a First in both Mods. and Greats and had begun reading the course in English literature. A particularly interesting feature of the English course was Professor George Gordon's discussion class. On the

9th February 1923 Lewis read a paper on Spenser to the class, the minutes of which, as I have mentioned elsewhere,[17] were written in Chaucerian verse by his friend Nevill Coghill. A few days later Lewis read the same paper to the Martlets. According to their minutes:

The 238th meeting of the society took place in Mr. Anderson's rooms on Wednesday Feb. 14th at 8 o'clock. Mr. C. S. Lewis read a brilliant paper on the poetry of Edmund Spenser. The paper included a comparison of Spenser with contemporary and antecedent facts and an interesting and compendious examination of his technique as regards vocabulary and metrical execution. Mr. Lewis gave it as his opinion that The Faerie Queene excelled Spenser's other works in any particular quality for which each is valued. Its unity—and it is an unity—comprises an extraordinary variety of materials. Perhaps none who has not done so by the age of seventeen, has ever succeeded in reading the Faerie Queene from beginning to end. To read it in selection is to lose one great delight, the delight of wandering in a forest rather than in a wood. The unique quality possessed by English poetry at its best, and perhaps by no other poetry, a quality that might be best expressed by the untranslatable Greek word γάνος, runs through all that Spenser has written. Space does not permit us to give a more detailed account of Mr. Lewis's paper, as it was the wish of members present that the ensuing discussion should be described in full.[18]

I shall not, however, give the Secretary's minutes of the discussion that followed. Lewis had previously said little more in his diary than that such and such a topic was discussed by the Martlets, but after reading his paper on Spenser he went home and wrote in his diary all he could remember of the discussion that followed it. As his account is fuller and, I expect, more accurate than the one in the Martlets minute books, I shall quote it. It might be considered too long for inclusion here, but as this book is about Lewis the speaker I feel it would be a pity to omit this engaging picture of Lewis, as it were, in action. As some of it might be difficult for the reader to understand, I shall mention a few facts about Lewis which I hope will make it clearer. (1) Since coming to Oxford, it had been Lewis's chief ambition to become a successful poet. He was at this time writing a narrative poem, *Dymer*, and at the same time annoyed that the *avant-garde* poems, such as those of T. S. Eliot, were becoming a serious rival to the kind of verse he loved best—long narrative poems such as *The Faerie Queene*. (2) Literary criticism was beginning to shift its emphasis from what the poem or novel actually *said* to vague hypotheses about meaning and to concentrate rather more on the author than on what he wrote. (3) Lewis had hitherto regarded literature as something rather private. Now that it was being shared with others, many of whom differed widely from him, he was beginning to have to defend his tastes and to clarify his critical opinions. Those who are familiar with his works of literary criticism will, I expect, find in this discussion some of his ideas about criticism just beginning to take form. The other Martlets with whom he is talking are Messrs. R. A. Rink, W. D. Robson-Scott, P. J. Terry, A. K. Hamilton Jenkin, G. E. Fasnacht, and Sir David Keir. If these gentlemen should ever read this, I hope they will forgive me the liberty of revealing their part in this discussion without first asking their permission. Here is what Lewis wrote:

I had, in my paper, applied Murray's view of Pindar to Spenser, i.e., he failed to be a great poet because he was only a poet. This presently led to an argument of which the skeleton was something like this.

RINK: 'Do you say that a work of art cannot be the greatest in kind if it is only art?'

SELF: 'Certainly.'

RINK: 'But can't it be judged and oughtn't it to be judged just as art?'

SELF: 'Well taking art as an expression it must be the expression of something: and one can't abstract the "something" from the expression.'

RINK: '—Stated Croce's position.' *

SELF: 'You can't judge it simply as expression, in practice. A lyric which perfectly expressed the pleasure of scratching would not really be judged equal to Lear.'

RINK: 'But it would be, quâ art.'

SELF: 'But not quâ thing.'

RINK: 'Perhaps not: but it could be criticized just as

* Benedetto Croce who wrote *Aesthetics as the Science of Expression and General Linguistics.*

art without reference to its further nature as thing and that is what Croce means.'

SELF: 'I suggest that the object of a work of art is not to be criticized but to be experienced and enjoyed. And that which appeals to the whole man must be greater than that which appeals to part of the man.'

RINK: 'I don't think so, provided the emotion of the artist is perfectly expressed.'

SELF: 'That's all right, if you consider the artist alone. But you forget that art is a social thing.'

ROBSON-SCOTT and RINK: (together) 'Oh no, certainly not, you can't mean that.'

SELF: 'Why not? Isn't the object of the artist to communicate his emotion?'

RINK: 'Oh! Then you make art not expression but communication?'

SELF: 'Yes. I'm sorry I said expression before. I mean communication.'

RINK: 'But is it not disinterested? Does the artist, while at work, think about an audience or about anything but perfect expression?'

SELF: 'No artist has ever taken that view. Why are all artists so eager to be understood? Why do they bother to alter their first drafts?'

RINK: 'To express more perfectly.'

TERRY: 'Mere jottings might be the most expressive of all—to the artist.'

SELF: 'The artist goes on altering phrases which are merely expressive to himself and hunting for those which will reproduce the right emotion in the audience.'

JENKIN: 'Yes, I agree with that.'

KEIR: 'Keats' first draft of the Nightingale was found scattered all over the garden: so he had no idea of communication.'

JENKIN: 'That was mere accident—carelessness.'

RINK: 'But how can the essence of art depend upon its being communicative? If an Athenian had written Wagnerian music it would have communicated nothing to his contemporaries but it would have been art.'

SELF: 'I don't mean what "happens to communicate" in fact: but what is "such as to be communicative", tho' of course mere accidents—e.g. a MS getting lost—may prevent it ever actually arousing the right emotion.'

FASNACHT: 'Potentially communicative?'

SELF: 'Yes, I suppose so.'

TERRY: 'But almost anything would be that. A mere sign would be communicative to a person who happened to have the same associations as the artist.'

RINK: 'No, communication won't do: it will have to be expression.'

SELF: 'What do you mean by expression, if you don't mean what is potentially communicative?'

RINK: 'I mean that which embodies the form of the artist's experience.'

SELF: 'Form in the Platonic sense?'

RINK: 'Not exactly—I mean like the form of a penny.'

SELF: 'That comes to the Platonic form. That which corresponds to the round form of the penny, in a pain say, is Painfulness. You don't mean that the expression of the particular pain is the concept of painfulness?'

RINK: 'There's a difference. There are many pennies but every emotion is unique.'

SELF: 'Well can you talk about form and content in a unique thing?'

RINK: 'Why not?'

SELF: 'Well take the *whole*. Is its form inside it or out and what happens in either case?'

FASNACHT: 'It is neither, it is diffused.'

SELF: 'Can you distinguish it in this case from the particular?'

FASNACHT: 'The difficulty comes not from the uniqueness of the Whole but from its Wholeness.'

RINK: 'In any case, I take back Form in that sense. I really think I mean the form you impose on the experience. As perception is the forming of sensation.'

SELF: 'But do you impose that. Isn't it given?'

RINK: 'Oh no—for instance I impose form on that lamp. If it was on the edge of vision it would have none.'

FASNACHT: 'But that isn't a mental operation, it's the turning of your head.'

SELF: 'Yes, the form depends on your body: but to you, as Mind, it's part of the given.'

(This led to a longish argument on 'sensations when not attended to'—were they sensations?—and so on to a discussion of the Ego. Did it exist when not filled by an object? Rink thought it did potentially. I trotted out my favourite argument about the potential being always resident in the lower actual, greatly to Fasnacht's amusement. Rink said the actual in which potential subjectivity resided was the spirit unknown in its essence. We then returned to our muttons.)

RINK: (Having abandoned the word Form as hopeless) 'The work of art is the crystallized emotion—the emotion made permanent.'

FASNACHT: 'Made permanent in whose mind?'

RINK: 'I mean potentially permanent.'

SELF: 'Doesn't that mean "capable of rearousing the original experience"?'

RINK: 'Well yes.'

SELF: 'Then the issue is that I think art is communication, you make it auto-communication?'

RINK: 'The work of art is capable of recreating the original experience but that is an accident of it.'

SELF: 'Well what is its essence?'

RINK: 'I don't think I can put it into words. What I object to is making its essence depend on the future and on its contingent success in reproducing the experience. I want to make it retrospectively what this makes it in the future.'

We all now agreed that we had a certain inkling of what he meant. I said this was certainly not what I meant by art: in fact it stood to art as Narcissus to Eros.[19]

To those familiar with Lewis's books on literary criticism, it may seem as though he and his friends are making very heavy weather of what could be said more simply. Yet, it was no doubt because of discussions such as this that he was later able to think and write with scintillating logic and clarity. Compare, for instance, what he says above about the 'something' which art expresses to this statement written thirty-odd years later:

> Whatever is true of the poem, it is quite clear that the words in it must mean. A word which simply 'was' and didn't 'mean' would not be a word. This applies even to Nonsense poetry. *Boojum* in its context is not a mere noise. Gertrude Stein's 'a rose is a rose' if we thought it was 'arose is arose', would be different.[20]

By the time Lewis next spoke to the Martlets he had taken a First in English Literature and was looking for a fellowship in philosophy. No fellowship was offered him but, by a stroke of good fortune, he was asked to deputize for his old philosophy tutor, E. F. Carritt, who was going to the United States to lecture for a year. As Lewis was still an atheist at this time (though not a materialist), it may interest readers to learn that he chose as the title for his first term's lectures in the University 'The Moral Good—its place among the values.' He was writing these lectures when, on the 18th June 1924, he read his next paper at the two hundred and fifty-sixth meeting of the Martlets. According to the Secretary:

> The minutes of the last meeting were read and carried; the President then called upon Mr. Lewis to read his paper on James Stephens. Mr. Lewis began

by congratulating himself on his entire ignorance of biographical detail and proceeded forthwith to a critical appreciation of his author's works; he first touched on his poetry, which he did not value very highly, and then passed to his prose works, quoting admirably and extensively from The Charwoman's Daughter, The Crock of Gold, The Demi-Gods, and The Deirdre, which last marked a new genre. The Society, very unfamiliar with the subject of the paper, elicited further quotations from the reader in lieu of discussion.[21]

That night Lewis wrote in his diary: 'My quotations from Stephens produced much mirth and I think I made some converts.'[22] By 'converts' he meant, I believe, fellow admirers of Stephens's mixture of mythology and theosophy. Some years later, however, Lewis took Stephens to task for attacking G. K. Chesterton, whom Lewis much admired.[23] Perhaps the most important detail of these minutes is Lewis's undisguised delight in being ignorant of Stephen's private life. If I guess aright, we have here the germ of Lewis's belief that a book ought to be judged on its own merits rather than as part of the writer's autobiography. We shall hear more of this a little later.

During the summer of 1924 Lewis was too busy writing lectures to keep a diary. Consequently, my only information comes from the letters to his father. His public speaking had, hitherto, been confined to the rather cosy Martlets meetings where he was among friends, but he was now writing lectures on philosophy for an audience he could only imagine. In August, 1924, he wrote to his father:

> I am plodding on with my fourteen lectures . . . I think I said before that I am not writing them IN EXTENSO, only notes. The extemporary element thus introduced is dangerous for a beginner, but READ lectures send people to sleep and I think I must make the plunge from the very beginning and learn to TALK, not to recite. I practise continually, expanding my notes to imaginary audiences.[24]

Many people have asked whether the lectures Lewis gave in 1924 are extant. They are. I have his notebooks before me as I write. Lewis decided in the end to write them *in extenso*, and I will here give an example from his introductory lecture on 'Innate Ideas'. He begins:

> To prove that an idea is innate it wd. not be sufficient (even if it were possible) to show that it is universal: we must demonstrate that its certainty 'ne vient que de ce qui est en nous'. Nor, again, does it follow that an idea is *not* innate because all men do not know of it: it may be *virtually* present, ready to come into consciousness at the proper stimulus. In this sense, indeed, all necessary truths are innate—discoverable in the resources of our own minds, tho some less easily than others. This is not simply to say that we have the *faculty* for knowing such truths: what we have is a faculty for finding them in our own minds . . .

Lewis seems to have enjoyed lecturing on philosophy and was prepared to settle down for life as a philosophy don if only he could secure a fellowship in one of the colleges. He applied for several during the spring of 1925. Finally, however, he went so far as to apply for a fellowship in English Language and Literature at Magdalen College. Oddly enough, the fellowship at Magdalen was the only one offered him. The offer—which meant a change from philosophy to English—was made to him on the morning of the 20th May 1925: that evening he read a paper at the two hundred and sixty-sixth meeting of the Martlets. Considering his new job, his topic seems very fitting:

The President called upon Mr. Lewis to read his paper on 'Boswell'. The reader began by pointing out that Boswell was usually dwarfed by the greatness of his subject & asked his hearers for one night, rather to relegate Johnson to the subordinate position of one of his characters & to consider Boswell as an artist & ask what is the secret of his greatness.

Few characters in literature are so well known as Johnson. For a comparison we do not turn to the heroes of biographies, but to the characters of fiction, to Jane Eyre, Falstaff & Pickwick. Johnson while purporting to have historical reality actually has the reality of art. We treat him as a living man, we quarrel with him & are reconciled again. All this is Boswell's work & yet he is not currently supposed to be a great man. The reader then discussed the village idiot theory of Boswell's charm & said that it accounted for some but not all. The clever use which Boswell makes of his own discomfitures & the occasions on which he himself triumphs are sufficient to discount it. Likewise the wisdom of [the] Johnson theory is disproved, for collections of verbatim sayings do not make books. Boswell in recording conversation showed both the unconscious selection of memory & the conscious selection of the great artist. The reader quoted passages showing the immense debt which Johnson owes to Boswell. The merit of the 'Life' is that more than any other work, whether of fiction or of history, it produces the illusion of life.

A lively discussion followed in which Johnson's hatred of Scotsmen was brought to the fore. The members of that race present retaliated by asserting Johnson to be the ideal Englishman. Personal combats were avoided.[25]

While I was his secretary, Lewis paid me the compliment of several times asking what I should like for him to write. Whenever I read the minutes above I upbraid myself for never having requested an essay on Boswell and Johnson. Now that the opportunity is lost, I realize how odd it is that, though Lewis often quotes both men in his books, he never gave us so much as an essay on either. What is worse, neither the manuscript of his paper on Boswell, nor the manuscripts of any of the other papers he had previously read to the Martlets, are extant.

He next addressed the Martlets at their three

hundred and eighteenth meeting on the 3rd March 1930. I find in the minutes that: 'C. S. Lewis, Esq., M.A. read a paper on "the personal heresy in poetics." A discussion followed which lasted over an hour.'[26]

That's all. The Martlets had a very indolent Secretary at the time. Fortunately, however, it seems that Lewis preserved the manuscript, for a few years later he published an essay, 'The Personal Heresy in Criticism' in *Essays and Studies*, vol. XIX (1934), which I suspect is essentially the same essay as that he read to the Martlets. The theme is one he had been chewing over since 1924 when he congratulated himself on being *entirely ignorant* of James Stephens's private life. The essay attracted the attention of Dr. E. M. W. Tillyard whose interpretation of *Paradise Lost* Lewis had called in question. This led to a courteous and searching series of exchanges between Lewis and Tillyard in which the essay he read to the Martlets became chapter one of a book they published together under the title, *The Personal Heresy: A Controversy*.[27]

In this essay Lewis attacked the notion that in reading a man's poems one steeps oneself in the poet's personality, and that a poet's 'life' and 'works' are simply two diverse expressions of a single quiddity. It is a richly reasoned essay, and one is struck by a quality eminently characteristic of Lewis's works—his sheer common sense. Take this passage, for instance.

Let it be granted that I do approach the poet; at least I do it by sharing his consciousness, not by studying it. I look with his eyes, not at him. He, for the moment, will be precisely what I do not see; for you can see any eyes rather than the pair you see with, and if you want to examine your own glasses you must take them off your own nose. The poet is not a man who asks me to look at *him*; he is a man who says 'look at that' and points; the more I follow the pointing of his finger the less I can possibly see of *him*. To be sure there are all sorts of difficult questions hanging over us. But for the moment let us thrust them aside. Whatever may turn out to be the whole truth, let us make fast, before we go a step farther, this aspect of the truth. To see things as the poet sees them I must share his consciousness and not attend to it; I must look where he looks and not turn round to face him; I must make of him not a spectacle but a pair of spectacles.[28]

Characteristic too of Lewis are passages in which, after slow and careful reasoning, a sudden impatience in his voice clears our head of nonsense. In one place he quotes some lines from Keats in which trees are described as 'green-rob'd senators of mighty woods'. No one, we feel, could be more patient in showing us that, though 'green-rob'd senators' might conjure up individual associations in each of us, it is our common knowledge of Europe and ancient Rome which makes it possible for us to understand the poem. And then: 'It is not relevant that Keats first read about senators (let us say) in a little brown book, in a room smelling of boiled beef, the same day that he pulled out a loose tooth.'[29]

By the time Lewis read his next paper to the Martlets in 1933, he had been converted to Christianity. He described himself as a 'reluctant convert',[30] and I see no reason not to believe him. There was much to surrender. Lewis seems to have parted with his time and money easily enough, but I know from talking with him how difficult it was for him to give up his old ambition of being a successful poet. I sometimes imagine he would have been happier had God slapped a ban on the writing of *any* verse whatsoever, than that long narrative poems should have to give way to modern *vers libre*. I have a notion that the words 'modern literature' as used in the minutes which follow mean, in particular, modern poetry. Sometime in the 1950's Lewis came to have a profound respect for T. S. Eliot, but when he read a paper at the three hundred and thirty-seventh meeting of the Martlets on the 23rd November 1933, there were few things he enjoyed less than Mr. Eliot's versifying. The Secretary records that:

Mr. C. S. Lewis read a paper on 'Is Literature an Art?' before ten members and seven visitors. Mr. Lewis's paper was erudite and witty, though distinctly reactionary. He began by defining art as 'a trained habit' and went on to differentiate between the fine arts—music and painting—and literature because the former could always be made to order, which a poem could not. Furthermore, all good literature tells a tale, which good music or pictures, as a rule, do not. He continued, at some length, to emphasize his point of view—that the tale —the thing said—was all-important in literature; it should not be judged aesthetically. Kipling, he said, often tells his tales perfectly, even though they are often foolish or morally wicked. This led Mr. Lewis to a virulent but not unamusing attack on 'modern' literature, which he sweepingly dismissed because 'it had nothing to say'. Technique has been exalted above matter and the result was 'indeed a waste land'.[31]

I can easily picture the look on Lewis's face as he boomed out these last words, a look which my friend Owen Barfield has so aptly described as one of Lewis's most distinctive mannerisms, which is 'a tendency to accompany some unusually challenging or provocative or epigrammatic remark by its outward opposite—a deliberately fixed and expressionless stare at his inter-locutor or his audience, which had somewhat the effect of "daring" them to laugh at or be shocked by it'. They were both dared and shocked is my guess, for the Secretary goes on to say that a 'lengthy' discussion took place but that 'Mr. Lewis added little to what he had already said and refused to be drawn into dis-cussion on modern poetry'.[32]

The Martlets were being entertained by a great many distinguished men at this time, some of whom were old members of the Society. In 1928 Stephen Spender, the poet, read a paper on 'The Artistic Temperament'. During the following year one of the founder members, Professor Ernest de Selincourt, returned to give a paper on 'The Art of Conversation'; and Mr. John Maud, a member of the Martlets, spoke on 'The Poetry of A. E. Housman'. Mr. Maud, now Lord Redcliffe-Maud and the present Master of University College, told me he remembers being at several meetings of the Society with Lewis. Sir Michael Sadleir, who was Master when Lewis was at University College, read a paper in February, 1931, on 'Bulwer-Lytton—The Man'. In May, 1931, Sir Maurice Bowra, the Warden of Wadham College since 1938, and one of the most entertaining men I have ever been in company with, gave an address on 'Alexander Blok'. In 1934, Sir Basil Blackwell read a paper on 'The World of Books', and in the same year Msgr. Ronald Knox spoke on 'Detective-Stories'. Another old member, Professor R. G. Collingwood, returned in 1936 to read a paper on 'Who was King Arthur?' Professor Nevill Coghill, whom Lewis had known since 1923, read two papers to the Society: one in 1938 on 'Kafka; or, You Can't Win' and the other in February, 1941 on 'The Notion of Antichrist'. A month later Lewis brought along his friend Charles Williams who spoke to the Martlets on 'The Christianity of Baron Corvo'.

When Lewis next spoke to the Martlets in 1937 he was more mellow than he had been when reading 'Is Literature an Art?' He was on his way towards becoming the most popular lecturer in the University, and the success he had missed as a poet had been partly compensated for by his famous book, *The Allegory of Love* (1936). It is worth noting that, after eighteen years, he was once more defending one of his favourite poets against the popular hatred and neglect of Romanticism. The Secretary recorded that at the three hundred and sixty-sixth meeting of the Martlets on the 5th November 1937:

> Mr. C. S. Lewis read a paper on 'William Morris' to an audience of 12 members and 6 guests; among whom we were pleased to welcome the Master.*
>
> Mr. Lewis began by discussing the element of Northern-ness which characterized much of William Morris' work, together with that matter-of-factness in expression, which he combined with a style that sometimes has in it much of the Johnsonian. All this is most clearly seen in Morris' treatment of love, of which Mr. Lewis proceeded to give us some illustrations. Morris has also been called 'the most irreligious of poets', and 'anima naturaliter pagana' would be an apt description, though in some of his longer poems a tendency to become almost 'theological' is marked. While retaining his matter-of-factness, he gave free play to invention and heralded the return of invention to literature. At this point as Mr. Lewis was quoting the words,
>
> > 'A silence to make audible
> > The murmur of formless and wailing thoughts'
>
> there came through the open window a riot of formless and wailing noise; no silence was necessary to make that Highland instrument audible, and a blush

* Sir Michael Sadleir.

was observed on the face of our ex-President. But Mr. Lewis found in Morris' prose works the answer to that wailing, which threatened to make his poetry too unreal. He merged the individual in the totalitarian, and could say 'The world is in me'. With this attitude we might compare that of the modern poets who sing of 'One cog in the singing golden hive'. The key to the understanding of Morris was to be found in the struggle within him between love for mortal life and longing for immortality; and Mr. Lewis suggested that, as a result of the mingling of these two elements, it was in William Morris that the poets of the Left and the poets of the Christian revival might find contact. This concluded a very interesting and extraordinarily well-written paper.[33]

How interesting and well-written this paper is the reader can judge for himself as Lewis published it with several other pieces under the title *Rehabilitations* (Oxford, 1939).[34] Lewis was usually too modest to talk about his own writings, but in an article written years later about something entirely different, he mentions it by way of illustration. 'Very early in my career,' he said, 'I had published a book of essays; and the one into which I had put most of my heart, the one I really cared about and in which I discharged a keen enthusiasm, was on William Morris.'[35]

World War II knocked the Martlets Society pretty well out of action. But not quite. Lewis, despite his heavy load of work in the University and the BBC broadcasts he was writing at this time, still found time for those Martlets who were not in uniform. I find in the minutes that: 'The 387th meeting of the Society was addressed by Mr. C. S. Lewis in Trinity Term 1940. He read a paper on "Psycho-analysis and literature".'[36]

I find it extraordinary that when a well-known man delivers a splendid paper to a small society the Secretary should write no more than that. But I would not be uncharitable: the Secretary was probably listening to what he had to say. Besides, the essay is published in several places and we can read it for ourselves.[37] In this paper Lewis attempts to solve some of the literary problems thrown up by Freud's *Introductory Lectures on Psycho-analysis.* As most people have some bee or another in their bonnet about psychiatry, it is refreshing to hear the matter thought out so carefully and fairly as Lewis does here. One of the problems discussed has to do with Freud's belief that what an artist can't get in the real world he tries to get by imagining or pretending to have. With his characteristic logic, and the most delicate humour, Lewis demolishes this tenet and ends up, as it were, putting the psychiatrist on the couch. What I have just this minute noticed is that this is the first essay I have written about in which Lewis draws many examples from his own life.

An Oxford term lasts eight weeks, and Trinity Term begins about the third week in April and ends about the third week in June. It was in Trinity Term of 1940 that Lewis spoke at the three hundred and eighty-seventh meeting of the Society. The War was closing in on the Martlets, and it was at the three hundred and

eighty-eighth meeting on the 14th November 1940—
about five months later—that Lewis read his next, and
last, paper to the Martlets Society. The Secretary
records that:

> The 388th meeting was held on Nov. 14 at 8.15
> p.m. in Mr. T. P. Horley's rooms. Members present
> included Mr. Carritt and Mr. Wheare.* Guests
> from Merton and Keble were also welcomed.
>
> Mr. C. S. Lewis read a paper on 'The Kappa
> element in Romance'. In Romance, which could
> be defined as that element concerned with events
> other than the everyday, two distinct elements
> could be discerned. First, that which produced
> excitement in adventure etc. Secondly, the kappa
> element. Kappa was chosen as a symbol without
> other significance, and as the initial letter in
> 'κρυπτόν'.† Mr. Lewis discovered five major forms of
> 'Kappa'. First some scene or character interesting
> above and beyond the story: some sharp reminder
> of the sense of mystery in daily life. Secondly, an
> introduction of the intimate in the middle of the
> unfamiliar: thus in 'The Wind in the Willows',
> animal life was used to illustrate domestic virtues.
> Thirdly, an element of surprise in the discovery of a
> prospect we had speculated on: its differences from
> our expectations: its reminder of something in our
> own lives. Fourthly, the fulfilment of prophecy:

* The late E. F. Carritt, Lewis's philosophy tutor, and Mr. (now Sir)
Kenneth Wheare, the former Rector of Exeter College.
† Which means 'the hidden element'.

destiny operating by means of human free will. Fifthly, what he called 'twists': the convergence of things normally far apart. Mr. Lewis illustrated the four elements of quest, transformation, rebirth and twist by a dream quoted by Jung.

In conclusion Mr. Lewis said that the question of 'inestimable spiritual importance' (Jung) was an open question. Of three views—first, the classical explanation as allegorical profundity; secondly, the explanation of it as escapism; and thirdly; the psychoanalytic—the second might be rejected as not dealing with the experience at issue, while the first and third might be synthesized.

Mr. Carritt opened an interesting discussion, in which some scepticism about the value of the new category was mingled with an enthusiastic presentation of numerous well-known or obscure writings and even experiences for acceptance or rejection as the genuine 'kappa' article.[38]

Roger Lancelyn Green tells me he heard Lewis read what was essentially the same essay to a literary society in Merton College, though there the title had been changed to 'The Kappa Element in Fiction'. Lewis continued to revise it until it finally became the celebrated essay published as 'On Stories' in *Essays Presented to Charles Williams* (Oxford, 1947).[39] I have read and compared the Martlets notes and the finished essay many times, and I am tempted to write at length about the obvious, and the not-so-obvious, changes which the Martlets version went through before it became the polished version published in 1947. But I do not feel the reader would thank me for *that*—especially at the tail-end of a long essay. Besides, he may do that for himself. I hope he will.

If he does he will understand one of my chief reasons for burrowing into the Martlets minute books and bringing out all I could discover of Lewis's participation in that small but fiercely energetic little society. Most readers will have heard of the Inklings—Lewis and his friends who met every Thursday night during term in his Magdalen College rooms to read and discuss one another's writings. It is my belief that, what those Thursday evenings were to men whose reputations were pretty well established, the fortnightly meetings in University College were, in some degree, to Lewis and his fellow members. When a Martlet read a paper, he was laying himself open to abuse as well as praise. (In 1895 'A fear was expressed that Mr. Legh was skating more often than a member of the Society may without imperilling his literary reputation.') [40] In their meetings the wind of criticism was seldom, it seems, tempered to the shorn lamb: I note that one reader halfway through the discussion of his paper rushed hurriedly out of the room. I do not say that the key—or anything like it—to Lewis's success can be traced straight back to the Martlets. But something can. I know it led to *more* than what Lewis may have expected when he wrote: 'If I am forgotten of all else, at least a specimen of my handwiriting will be preserved to posterity.'

TO THE ROYAL AIR FORCE

STUART BARTON BABBAGE

Chapter Three

TO THE ROYAL AIR FORCE

STUART BARTON BABBAGE

'An inquisitiveness into the minutest circumstances and casual sayings of eminent contemporaries,' Coleridge testified, 'is indeed quite natural: but so are all our foibles.' This must be my justification for seeking to record, after the lapse of a quarter of century, my memories of C. S. Lewis as Lay Lecturer on the Staff of the Chaplains' Department of the Royal Air Force.

I do not know the details of his appointment as honorary lecturer: whether the Chaplain-in-Chief took the initiative in relation to his appointment or whether Lewis offered his services. At a chaplains' conference in London, in the fall of 1941, we were informed by the Chaplain-in-Chief that C. S. Lewis would be available at weekends to speak on the Christian faith.

I wrote inviting him to speak to the men of the heavy bomber squadrons in Norfolk with whom I was serving. Our casualties had been heavy: we were, at the time, engaged in massive night bombing attacks against some of the most heavily fortified targets in Germany and occupied Europe. A tour of duty consisted of thirty or more operations against enemy targets: after that, a man was taken off for a period of rest before being scheduled for another tour. The grim fact was that, on the average, a man only completed thirteen raids before being killed or posted missing. These men (in the glory of their budding manhood) knew, statistically speaking, that there was little chance of their completing even one tour.

Lewis's answer from Oxford came by return mail. Closely handwritten, it was on the corner of a piece of torn paper. Yes, he would be glad to come, and he would arrive by train on Saturday morning.

Lewis apparently felt that the best contribution he could make, as a citizen and as a Christian, was to explain to those who were prepared to listen what the Christian faith is all about. It was characteristic of him that he should add to his official academic responsibilities this time-consuming assignment as his own form of 'war work'.

For Lewis these speaking engagements meant time snatched away from his writing. During the course of the weekend, I learned that he was already immersed in the writing of a novel: of course, he explained, a *theological* novel. On 11th May 1942 he informed a friend: 'The Venus book is now finished except that I find the first two chapters need re-writing.'[1]

C. S. Lewis was convinced that imaginative writing can be used in the service of the faith. Any amount of theology, he explained, can be smuggled into people's minds under the guise of fiction and romance.[2] The advantage of science fiction as a medium is that it deals with far deeper and more serious issues than realistic fiction—with cosmic issues and the ultimate problems of human destiny. 'I grew up,' he later told a friend, 'on the works of H. G. Wells: but it was David Lindsay's *Voyage to Arcturus* which gave me the idea that the appeal of science might be used in the service of supernatural religion.'[3]

During the weekend we had opportunities for much good talk. He disliked intensely meaningless gossip—the endless repetition of isolated and unrelated bits of casual information. What he relished, he frequently testified, was 'the cut and parry of prolonged, fierce, masculine argument . . .'.[4] He was bored by mere facts: what stimulated him was the vigorous exchange of ideas and opinions and views.

Lewis had served as a combatant in World War I (being wounded in the final German assault on the Western Front). He had no doubt that Hitler was an evil genius and that we were right to fight. He also detested Stalin as a sadistic tyrant: he felt that our best hope was that Germany and Russia would systematically destroy each other. I was not prepared for this blunt expression of the philosophy of power politics from the lips of a professing Christian, and I was profoundly shocked.

In my bedroom, soon after his arrival, I proudly showed him some of the works of Sören Kierkegaard. He had never heard of him. I was passing through a stage of youthful and eager enthusiasm for the works of the melancholy Dane, and I brashly proceeded to enlighten him. I expatiated at length on Kierkegaard's life and thought, relating, in some detail, the circumstances under which Kierkegaard had driven Regina Olsen to break their engagement by representing himself to be a seducer and a deceiver.

Kierkegaard had meditated deeply on the significance of God's command to Abraham to sacrifice his son Isaac: was he, in relation to his own prospective marriage, being called upon to sacrifice the one he loved? Lewis had had enough. 'Tell me no more,' he brusquely interjected; 'the man was pathological.' And he refused to hear any more.

I had the pastoral oversight of two aerodromes two or three miles apart. Each Sunday, after an early morning celebration of Holy Communion, I conducted two parade services, often in the open air. I also held an evening service in the small but austerely beautiful timbered chapel that had been presented to the Royal Air Force by an engineering firm specializing in the manufacture of aeroplane turrets. The chapel had been formally opened by King George VI, only a few months previously.

We discussed the details of the Sunday services. He strongly disapproved of parade services in general and of compulsory church attendance in particular. I justified them as necessary evil, given the conditions under which we lived and worked, but he was inflexible. They were wrong, and he objected on principle to regimented religion. Parade services were calculated, he firmly believed, to harden men in impenitence.

Lewis was a formidable controversialist. He had a kind of Johnsonian pugnacity, but, though aggressive, he was not offensive. He expressed himself vigorously and emphatically, but always in the context of great good humour. He was, in Austin Farrer's apt phrase, 'a bonny fighter'.[5] His dogmatism was the product of a burning honesty; he was incapable, intellectually or morally, of evasion or equivocation. 'We have both learnt our dialectic,' he reminded E. M. W. Tillyard (in the course of a celebrated academic debate on the nature of poetry), 'in the rough academic arena where knocks that would frighten the London literary coteries are given and taken in good part.'[6] Concerning Lewis, Tillyard generously acknowledged that 'he is the best kind of opponent, good to agree with when one can, and for an enemy as courteous as he is honest and uncompromising; the kind of opponent with whom I should gladly exchange armour after a parley, even if I cannot move my tent to the ground where his own is pitched'.[7]

During the course of his visit, he occupied a guest room in the Officers' Mess. The Mess was full of air crew members who, later that evening, would leave the security of the base for bombing attacks on selected enemy targets. After briefing instructions and prior to take-off, the lounge was unnaturally quiet: the men, sitting apart, silently preoccupied, clammily sweating, knowing the target, and dreading the outcome. Across the Channel, there was, they knew only too well, a waiting holocaust of terror.

We talked about the fact of death. Every day there were planes shot down or planes that did not return, and every day there were next-of-kin to whom letters of comfort and condolence had to be written. In the intimacy of my room, a man would suddenly blurt out: 'Padre, I don't want to die!' These men, in the pride of their superb physical manhood, were pathetically eager to stay alive. They had suddenly become aware of the palpable presence of death and of the implacable beauty of life. They desperately wanted to live and to know what it is to love and be loved.

We discussed the difference that the Christian faith makes to the life of a man in relation to the fact of death. Christianity does not, of course, exempt a man from the slings and arrows of outrageous fortune (it is no insurance policy); what it gives, I argued, is a sense of inner peace, of confident trust, of quiet assurance. Lewis disagreed. No, he said, death is dreadful and we are right to fear it. I quoted some of the familiar passages of Scripture: the confidence of the shepherd Psalmist that, though a man walk through the valley of the shadow of death, he need fear no evil because God is with him, and the apostle Paul's triumphant boast that neither death nor life is able to separate us from the love of God which is in Christ Jesus our Lord. I referred to Dr. Edward Wilson, who, in his last farewell letter to his wife, written from the frozen wastes of Antarctica, testified that death had no terrors and that death was a very little thing. Lewis was of a different opinion: death, he replied, is not a very little thing and it is horrible.

Lewis had a healthy detestation of religious cant. He clearly distrusted my comfortable and confident pietism, my glib resolution of life's enigmas, my easy assurance in the presence of death. My attitude, he implied, was sentimental rather than serious; and I was not honestly facing what death really is.

Twenty years later, he wrote a poignant little book about his own feelings at the time of his wife's death. 'If you're approaching God,' he noted, 'not as the goal but as a road, not as the end but as a means, you're not really approaching Him at all. That's what was really wrong with all those popular pictures of happy reunions "on the further shore"; not the simple-minded and very earthly images, but the fact that they make an End of what we can get only as a by-product of the true End.' [8]

I confess that I subsequently found some measure of satisfaction in the fact that when he came to die, he was able to speak of the experience as rather 'solemn fun'. He related:

> I was unexpectedly revived from a long coma and perhaps the almost continuous prayers of my friends did it—but it wd. have been a luxuriously easy passage, and one almost regrets having the door shut in one's face. Ought one to honour Lazarus rather than Stephen as the protomartyr? To be brought back and have all one's dying to do again was rather hard. When you die, and if 'prison visiting' is allowed, come down and look me up in Purgatory. It *is* all rather fun—solemn fun—isn't it? [9]

But I have digressed from the sequence of my story. On Sunday he attended the early service of Holy Communion, and then, after breakfast, he spoke at the main aerodrome, repeating his address later at the satellite station.

He cleverly caught the attention of his audience by the topicality of his opening illustration. 'I remember once,' he began, 'when I'd been giving a talk to the R.A.F., an old, hard-bitten officer got up and said, "I've no use for all that stuff. But, mind you, I'm a religious man too. I *know* there's a God. I've *felt* Him: out alone in the desert at night: the tremendous mystery. And that's just why I don't believe all your neat little dogmas and formulas about Him. To anyone who's met the real thing they all seem so petty and pedantic and unreal!"' [10]

Lewis conceded that for that officer, the experience of God in the desert was far more real than the traditional and time-honoured language of the Christian creeds. 'In the same way, if a man has once looked at the Atlantic from the beach, and then goes and looks at a map of the Atlantic, he also will be turning from something more real to something less real: turning from real waves to a bit of coloured paper. . . . As long as you're content with walks on the beach, your own glimpses are far more fun than looking at a map. But the map's going to be more use than walks on the beach if you want to get to America.' And theology, he pointedly concluded, is like a map.

As an apologist, Lewis knew how important it is to begin with that which is known before plunging into that which is unknown. It is important, he believed, not to despise that which a man already knows by experience to be true. It is valid as far as it goes, and it provides a base on which to build. 'Doctrines,' he pointed out, 'aren't God: they're only a kind of map. But that map's based on the experience of hundreds of people who really were in touch with God—experiences compared with which any thrills or pious feelings you and I are likely to get on our own are very elementary and very confused.' If you want to get any further, he repeated, you've got to use a map.

Christianity, he went on, tells us about another world, about something *behind* the world we can touch and hear and see. Christianity tells us that we can become sons of God. 'This world,' he finally concluded, 'is a great sculptor's shop. We are the statues and there is a rumour going round the shop that some of us are some day going to come to life.'

It is worth noting, from a study of the published text, some of the devices Lewis employed to achieve an effect of telling immediacy. To begin with, he consistently rooted his subject matter in the known experience of his hearers. Secondly, he deliberately adopted an idiomatic style of speaking as nearly as possible related to the conventions and patterns of ordinary conversation. He used words that are direct and simple and crystal clear. He did not hesitate to appropriate the accepted abbreviations of conversational speech: contractions like 'you've' for 'you have' and 'map's' for 'map is'. He studiously avoided being pompous or pedantic: particularly the use of abstract terms, meaningless technical jargon and intimidating polysyllabic Latinisms. He aimed at conciseness and compression and clarity, and he achieved it. His language was uniformly spare and economical and the argument was always taut. Thirdly, he recognized the illustrative and interpretive value of the apt metaphor and the striking image. Fourthly, he instinctively appreciated the importance of empathy and self-identification. He knew how to disarm his hearers by placing himself on the same level as those to whom he spoke. 'The feelings you and I are likely to get on our own,' he reminded them, 'are very elementary and very confused.' It was characteristic of him that he should include himself.

Lewis was emphatic that he was neither a professional theologian nor a clergyman. He was, he insisted, a 'mere Christian'. To emphasize his lay status, he preferred, when preaching, to wear an ordinary suit rather than some form of official dress. He was singularly uninterested in matters of ecclesiastical haberdashery, and he had no sympathy with fussy ritual. It was sufficient that I was decently arrayed, as in duty bound, in my cassock and surplice, hood and scarf.

He spoke without notes. His voice, which was naturally rich and resonant, carried well in the open air. There was, of course, no amplification to cause distortion and create distraction; he was spared that final indignity. He spoke without affectation and without exaggeration, as one would expect an educated Englishman to speak.

He was not naturally impressive: his clothes were rumpled and invariably creased; he was short and stocky and almost pudgy; his face, which was full, was florid; his eyes had the appearance of being puffy and distended. He spoke easily and fluently, without hesitation, and without gestures.

The circumstances, however, were not conducive to good communication. The majority of the men were impressed, but they were not, as the contemporary phrase has it, particularly 'turned on'. An address which relies on logic and close reasoning (no matter how persuasively presented) is bound to lose much of its cogency and power when delivered in the empty vastness of the open air. Lewis was accustomed to the reassuring intimacy and the easy rapport of the lecture hall and found himself at a disadvantage when called upon to address an audience of indifferent servicemen. He confessed to a friend (in a letter dated 15th May 1941): 'I've given talks to the RAF at Abingdon already, and so far as I can judge, they were a complete failure. . . .'[11]

In the afternoon we went walking across the fens of Norfolk. I commented on his willingness to spend time and energy travelling across the length and breadth of England to undertake this kind of itinerant ministry. He felt that it was worth it to bring encouragement to some lonely chaplain who had been finding the going hard. As his published correspondence reveals, and as this conversation indicates, he had a pastor's heart and a vast charity.

We discussed the prospective programme for the evening service. He indicated that what he personally desired in church services were fewer, better, and shorter hymns, but especially fewer. Later I came across confirmations of this in his autobiography

Surprised by Joy: 'Hymns were (and are) extremely disagreeable to me,' he confesses.[12] His aversion was partly literary and partly personal. Most hymns are an unhappy mixture of pretentious piety and maudlin sentiment, and most popular hymn tunes are banal and undistinguished. I feelingly recalled the contribution of William Cowper and Charles Wesley and Isaac Watts, but he was in no mood for compromise, and I did not press the point.

There were, I guessed, personal reasons for his strong antipathy. Public worship was, for him, a duty rather than a delight. It was a matter of discipline and obedience. In his autobiography, he argues with some passion, that worship ought to be 'a matter of good men praying alone and meeting by twos and threes to talk of spiritual matters'. A normal church service irritated and exasperated him. He objected to 'the fussy, time-wasting botheration of it all! the bells, the crowds, the umbrellas, the notices, the bustle, the perpetual arranging and organizing'.[13] He had, I concluded, been unfortunate in his experience of institutional religion. He frankly recognized that part of the fault was in himself. 'I have,' he admitted, 'a sort of spiritual *gaucherie* which makes me unapt to participate in any rite.'[14]

I wanted him to have some idea about the character and composition of the evening congregation. Those present, I reassured him, would be there by their own will and volition. There would be no conscripts. The majority would be officers rather than airmen. It was not an easy thing for an airman to separate himself from the close communal life of the barracks for the purpose of going to church. John Stuart Mill once observed that there is a social tyranny which can be a more subtle and ubiquitous enemy to liberty than any political despotism. Many an airman, during the days of World War II, was made acutely aware of a subtle and ubiquitous social tyranny that was inimical to the overt expression of any idiosyncratic belief or practice. Only a select few had the moral strength and stamina to withstand the suffocating tyranny of barracks life and the deadly pressure to conform.[15]

The situation in the Officers' Mess was very different. Church-going among members of the middle class—the class to which most of the officers belonged —is still a badge of conventional respectability (although increasingly more honoured in the breach than in the observance). There are, of course, a number of sociological reasons for this. The church, it has been rightly said, has not lost the working class: the working class was never in it. Since the days of the industrial revolution, the church's impact on the working class has been minimal. Perhaps there is also something inherently dehumanizing about life lived in service to the machines of modern industry.

I repeated that attendance for some of these men would be costly and difficult. 'It might be helpful,' he quietly replied, 'if I told them something of what it costs *me* to be a Christian.'

The chapel was uncomfortably crowded. The platform, above the entrance, which had to be reached by a perpendicular ladder, was also filled. The lectern from which I conducted the service had pieces of shrapnel embedded in the wood, historic mementoes of a low-level machine-gun attack by some daring German pilots during the Battle of Britain.

Lewis stood in the aisle, a dishevelled and dumpy figure in a baggy suit. Having invoked the Name of the Father, the Son, and the Holy Spirit, he announced his text: 'If any man will come after me, let him deny himself, and take up his cross, and follow me.'

He spoke of what Jesus endured on our behalf: misunderstanding and loneliness and finally betrayal and death. He vividly painted the scene in the judgment hall: the soldiers, baiting and buffeting Him; Herod, mocking and deriding Him; the disciples, forsaking and denying Him. And then he recalled, with graphic power, the horror of the crucifixion scene.

Lewis told us what it had cost him, as an Oxford don, to be a Christian. One might have expected to find within a university environment, and particularly at Oxford University, that home of lost causes, some measure of tolerance and liberality, some recognition and acceptance of the sanctity of honest belief and sincere conviction. Lewis discovered, as others have discovered before and since, that in this world there are few persons so illiberal as those who claim to be liberal and few persons so irrational as those who claim to be rational. His liberal and rational friends, he explained, did not object to his intellectual interest in Christianity; it was, they agreed, a proper subject for academic argument and debate; but to insist on seriously practising it—that was going too far. He did not mind being accused of religious mania, that familiar gibe of the natural man; what he was unprepared for was the intense hostility and animosity of his professional colleagues. Within the academic community, he unexpectedly found himself an object of ostracism and abuse. (Major W. H. Lewis confirms that his brother's conversion had 'various consequences', among which, he admits, was 'hostility in some quarters'.[16] He had not been prepared for such virulent hostility: he could understand impatience but not indignation, criticism but not ostracism.

Lewis related these hurtful personal memories for the sake of those who were also finding the living of the Christian life difficult. He knew, he told them, what it is to endure scornful ridicule and the opprobrium of intellectual contempt; he knew what it is to have one's motives questioned and one's actions misinterpreted. At home, his desire to attend early service was represented as a selfish desire to inconvenience the other members of the household; it was clear, they said, that he was becoming a fanatic and losing all sense of proportion.

He spoke once again of the calumnies and indignities that Christ endured. With deep feeling and burning passion, he described the wanton cruelty of the soldiers as they shouted angrily: 'That's him!' 'Hypocrite!' 'Serves him right!' 'That's what he deserves!' 'Dirty traitor!' And, as he evoked the horror and the hate, he suited his action to his words, vigorously gesticulating.

It is not surprising that he 'communicated', for this was powerful preaching, born of intense and passionately felt emotion.

Despite the moving nature of the subject matter, his style of speaking was personal rather than oratorical. He spoke earnestly and emphatically. In this address we were, once again, made aware of his extraordinary feeling for words, of his rare ability to use exactly the right word in the right place, and of the endless fertility of his imagination.

Cicero (according to the testimony of Augustine) laid it down as an axiom that 'he who is eloquent should speak in such a way that he teaches, delights, and moves. Then he added, "To teach is a necessity, to please is a sweetness, to persuade is a victory." '27 Judged by these criteria, Lewis had the gift of natural eloquence in abundant measure. Like the Roman orator of antiquity, he was eager to present his case, to plead its merits, and to demand a verdict.

And this is what he did, with consummate skill, on one unforgettable night during the days of World War II, when he spoke to a select congregation of officers and other ranks in an Air Force Chapel in the lonely wastes of the Norfolk fens.

IN THE UNIVERSITY

GEORGE BAILEY

Chapter Four

IN THE UNIVERSITY

GEORGE BAILEY

My first meeting with C. S. Lewis in January, 1946, was prejudiced as far as I was concerned by the fact that it was he, and none other, who was to decide whether I would be accepted as an undergraduate by Magdalen College. This was because Lewis was at that time at the height of his fame: he had far more students than he could conveniently handle in a college already over-crowded with the backlog of the war years.

It is difficult to reconstruct and almost impossible to exaggerate Lewis's prestige in postwar Oxford. Lewis was Lewis. His repute as a Christian apologist, as a popularizer-philosopher-theologian was extraordinary. His pre-eminence in the field of English letters in the university was unique. There was Coghill, there was Lord David Cecil, there were Wrenn, and C. T. Onions, but they were all, however impressive in themselves, only foothills in the shadow of the towering grandeur of Lewis. To have C. S. Lewis as tutor was universally regarded as an awesome honour. 'What? you are reading English at Magdalen; that means that C. S. Lewis is your tutor!' The prospect of spending an hour every week closeted with the most eminent scholar in his field was eclipsed only by the terror of having to read an essay for his criticism—to expose one's puny efforts to the full force of perhaps the most powerful and best-trained intellect in the world.

In his rooms in the New Building (erected *c*. 1640) overlooking a superb expanse of closely cropped lawn, which serves as a bowling green, I found a medium-size, rather stout, ruddy-faced man with a fine, large head (what the Germans call a 'Charakterkopf'), and a booming voice much given to what someone once called 'rhetorical guffawing' ('Ho, ho, ho, so you think Milton was ascetic, do you? Ho, ho! You are quite wrong there!'). Lewis looked—and often acted—like the school book description of Friar Tuck. His general manner was pronouncedly and—it often seemed—deliberately hearty. But he displayed no heartiness during my first interview with him. Just as I was about to take my leave, Lewis said to me: 'Are you aware, sir, that your fly is open?' My surprise was so great that it precluded embarrassment: 'If I had been, sir, I should never admit it.'

It was widely rumoured that Lewis did not like Americans. One of the causes for his distaste, allegedly, was that his very popularity in America expressed itself in thousands of fan letters and, still more embarrassing for Lewis, food packages. Even in England's severest austerity period, no Oxford don was ever in direct need of supplementary victuals. Lewis grumbled that I was 'a bit long in the tooth' (but then so were most of the ex-service men). He also questioned whether, as an

American, I had sufficient background in English literature to undertake the course. He suggested, in fact, that I take the alternate course, with the emphasis on language and etymology, rather than on literature. I declined. Lewis nevertheless accepted me.

The Oxford and Cambridge tutorial system is based, as it were, on the direct confrontation of tutor and undergraduate. The form of the system is simple: one essay a week on a set topic, which is read aloud by the undergraduate to the tutor during an hour long tutorial. Ordinarily the reading of the essay takes up the first fifteen minutes of the hour. In the remaining time, the tutor attacks the essay's argument or lack of one, and the undergraduate does his best to defend his work. I learned from Lewis long after leaving Oxford that his greatest dread in tutorials was the poor student who was also laconic. Such a student's essay would take only five or six minutes of the hour; it would take perhaps another four or five minutes to dispense with it, leaving fifty minutes of petrifying boredom. As far as I know, no undergraduate ever dared appear for a tutorial with Lewis with his essay only half finished. In such a case, the undergraduate would plead last minute indisposal and leave the great man in peace. I remember one occasion when my partner in a tutorial (to deal with the unwonted number of students, tutors would sometimes take undergraduates in tandem, each writing an essay on alternate weeks) defaulted at the last minute, and I found myself alone with Lewis with no essay since it was my week off. Lewis clearly expected me to take my leave. But I could not forbear to remain for the full hour and talk with Lewis. When I left he thanked me for 'a very interesting hour of talk'. For my part I was disappointed: I had fervently hoped to benefit from his lore in reply to several burning questions. Instead I was informed—or rather left to infer—that I had no real notion of the categories of thought, that what I took to be ethical questions were in reality moral questions, etc. Lewis was always either forming or guarding the definition.

Lewis had three standard forms of comment on an essay. If the essay was good: 'There is a good deal in what you say.' If the essay was middling: 'There is something in what you say.' If the essay was bad: 'There *may* be something in what you say.' His other fairly standard comments were: 'Too much straw and not enough bricks,' and, 'Not with Brogans, please, slippers are in order when you proceed to make a literary point.' Lewis was sparing of his compliments—the highest I know of was 'Much of that was very well said'—but he was quick to notice any excellence of usage. He spent five minutes praising one word I had used to describe Dryden's poetry (the word was 'bracing').

But the most important point about the tutorial system in general and Lewis's use of it in particular is that 'what you *say*' is either 'well *said*' or not. For the essay is always read aloud. In three years at Oxford, an undergraduate will write from fifty to seventy-five essays. The most important thing about having to read an essay aloud regularly is that it forces the undergraduate to write for reading aloud. Because he himself has to do the reading aloud, he soon becomes aware that he must make punctuational allowances for breathing pauses, which is perhaps the best way (because it is the most rudimentary way) to come to an understanding of sentence structure. The undergraduate must write so that when he reads aloud his tutor will understand without being obliged to request the repetition of a sentence or a phrase. It is understood that a request for the repetition of a passage is fatal. As far as I know, Lewis simply declined to request repetition. If the essay was not clear in the first reading, then it was unclearly written. The rule holds good generally: if the reader is forced to reread a sentence to enable the listener to understand it, it is almost certainly a case of bad writing or, at least, dull writing.

In writing for the ear rather than for the eye, immediate intelligibility is the first commandment, but it is not the only commandment. It is also necessary to get your listener's interest and then keep it. Lewis was a master in the art of putting things pungently, of forming and timing statements so that they were unforgettable. These were certainly the qualities that distinguished him as a university lecturer. While I was at Oxford, he was by far the most popular lecturer at the university. His lecture series 'Prolegomena to Renaissance Poetry' always attracted overflow crowds. As the title of the series suggests, Lewis's approach to the subject was classical. He harped on the necessity for going back to the classical Greek and Latin authors for an understanding of the Renaissance period. His harping was beautifully insistent. One of his general comments in this vein was quoted throughout the university for years on end: 'To die without having read the *Symposium* would be ridiculous—it would be like never having bathed in the sea, never having drunk wine, never having been in love.' Undergraduates quoting this statement usually substituted an aposiopesis for the last three words, a trailing off that ended in a loud clearing of the throat.

This sort of trick was far beneath Lewis who never noticeably strove for effect. Indeed, his delivery in his lectures was entirely straightforward, almost severe. He never noticeably consulted his lecture notes. When he had finished his lecture, he folded up his papers almost as he uttered the last word and walked briskly in a beeline for the door. No one would have dared accost him in his passage. He was blessed with a fine, sonorous baritone voice capable of a wide range of intonation and inflection. But his delivery was highly disciplined and deceptively easy. He was never dramatic, let alone melodramatic. I cannot remember a single gesture during his lectures. In appearance at the rostrum he was relaxed, almost deadpan, a study in economy. He was the consummate medium for what he had to say: he gave every word, every phrase, every sentence, every larger passage its full value. He gave full expression to his flashes of humour without obtruding his personality, as it were, between the flash and the audience. His style, I suppose, was low pressure but never conspicuously so. Lewis, I am sure, never 'threw away a line' in his life. Here is an example from the 'Prolegomena': 'Reason can see truth in sleep with three kinds of clarity: . . . in the oracle kind (oraculum) some venerable person (an ancestor, wise-man, parent, or even a tutor) appears and announces truth otherwise unknown.' The laugh from the audience came after the words 'even a tutor' which in Lewis's delivery were neither emphasized nor de-emphasized. In short, Lewis was perfectly discreet. But it was here in his lectures, strangely enough, that one became aware of an agreeable sensation of personal warmth. It was here, too, that one sensed the Promethean passion.

The exposure to direct, individual, personal relationships necessitated by the tutorial system produces a paradox. It accounts, I think, for the stand-offishness of most dons outside the tutorials (living together within the rather narrow confines of the college walls is, of course, part and parcel of the system). As a result, with few exceptions, dons have little or nothing to do with undergraduates. Socializing between the two groups is held to an absolute minimum. And small wonder. A don who cultivated his students socially would have little time for anything else. Lewis, as behooved a man of his well-nigh prodigious literary and scholarly production, carefully husbanded his time. He warded off private dinner invitations by pleading a glandular condition that became acute and unsightly during digestion. He did not have the disease, he explained, only all the symptoms. He did not live in college, he and his brother keeping a large house—which none of us ever saw—on a hill overlooking Oxford from the east. Lewis crossing Magdalen bridge in the morning—always at a brisk pace and with the cane the peripatetic Englishman always affects—was a familiar sight.

Lewis seldom if ever played the preceptor. But he himself was so well-organized that he had no sympathy with the undergraduate who stayed up all night on the eve of his tutorial to finish (or start and half finish) his essay. He would pontificate on this one point: 'You don't have to work hard if you work steadily—only innately lazy men are hard workers.'

He would try, on rare occasions, to teach his pupils how to think: 'one little squiggle goes up (to the surface of the mind) and is rejected. Then another little squiggle goes up and is rejected, and so on until a squiggle finally is accepted as valid. This is the thought process.' In discussing essays, particularly in arguing points of philosophy or aesthetics, Lewis would always use analogy—the metaphor in syllogistic harness—to solve all problems. He did this sort of thing instinctively; it was his method of 'picture thinking' which he used so extensively in his books. This is hardly surprising since his major scholastic feat was his acquisition of a pano-ramic insight into the nature of allegory. Judging from the following, which is the key passage of *The Allegory of Love*, the insight must have seemed to Lewis to constitute a universal pass-key:

But to be thus conscious of the divided will is necessarily to turn the mind in upon itself. . . . it is plain that to fight against 'Temptation' is also to explore the inner world; and it is scarcely less plain that to do so is to be already on the verge of allegory.

We cannot speak, perhaps we can hardly think, of an 'inner conflict' without a metaphor; and every metaphor is an allegory in little. And as the conflict becomes more and more important, it is inevitable that these metaphors should expand and coalesce, and finally turn into the fully-fledged allegorical poem. It would be a misunderstanding to suggest that there is another and better way of representing that inner world, and that we have found it in the novel and the drama. The gaze turned inward with a moral purpose does not discover *character*. No man is a 'character' to himself, and least of all while he thinks of good and evil. Character is what he has to produce; within he finds only the raw material, the passions and emotions which contend for mastery. That unitary 'soul' or 'personality' which interests the novelist is for him merely the arena in which the combatants meet: it is to the combatants —those 'accidents occurring in a substance'—that he must attend. Nor will he long attend to them . . . without giving them their Hegelian 'hands and feet'. For such a man allegory will be no frigid form.[1]

For such a man, allegory, or 'allegory in little'—the constant, systematic use of metaphor and simile, 'picture thinking'—became the *modus operandi* for his life work—in his speech as well as in his writing. Indeed, as a tutor Lewis worked this method to the point of annoyance. I remember the complaint of Ken Tynan, then the most flamboyant, if not the most illustrious, undergraduate in the college: 'He is eternally trotting out his damned figures in tutorials—"Now if you have three apples and I have five bananas. . . ." It's always three apples and five bananas, and no cigar. He's casuistic.'

But Tynan's opinion of Lewis mellowed with the years. Not long ago he told me about a BBC television appearance of Lewis's. A programme director who specialized in candid, unprepared interviews asked Tynan if he thought Lewis would agree to appear on his programme. 'He might,' said Tynan, 'but you won't catch him out: he'll get round you, mark my words.' The prediction was borne out royally. After a certain amount of sparring, the interviewer sprang his big question: 'As *the* authority on *The Allegory of Love*, Mr. Lewis, what is your attitude to the detailed, non-allegorical description of the act of love in literature?' 'To describe the act of love in detail without resorting to allegory,' answered Lewis, 'one is restricted to three choices: the language of the nursery, the language of the gutter, or the language of science—all are equally unsatisfactory.'

As a tutor Lewis was interesting, colourful, and lively, but he was not a good teacher. I do not consider this a very serious charge against Lewis. Good teachers are extremely rare. In twenty years of schooling, I consider it my great good fortune to have encountered two good teachers. Lewis did not have the gift of imparting enthusiasm. This was not because he did not believe in enthusiasm, although he disliked effulgence. He had his own brand of Promethean fire. I remember once complaining to him that I was bewildered and dismayed by the amount of knowledge I had acquired so quickly and the amount I still had to acquire. 'Do not be,' said Lewis. 'The human mind has no limits of capacity. It will take as much as you give it. It will stretch to embrace any amount of knowledge.'

But Lewis lacked the warmth to fire his students with enthusiasm. He lacked even the active interest in developing their capacities. He took his students as they came and took care only to make sure that they met the basic requirements to pass schools. Either he was not a very good judge of character or his lack of interest in his students prevented him from assessing them accurately. From the very first tutorial, for example, Lewis consistently mistook me for Geoff Dutton, an Australian and an excellent student, and Dutton for me. My weak protests and Dutton's strong ones were equally and utterly in vain. For three years I basked in my misgiven status of a talented dominion-ite while Dutton groaned in durance vile as the only American in the college—if not, indeed, in the university—with the temerity to read English. And this despite the difference in quality of performance. In a sort of psychological swing arrangement, Lewis credited Dutton's performances to me and penalized Dutton for mine.

After schools Lewis confessed that he had been much surprised when Robert Browning had scored the only first class honours in English in the college. 'I thought he was a bit too silly to make a first,' said Lewis. But in point of fact, Browning was the only one among us who was not afraid to betray his ignorance by asking questions so basic that they were bound to seem silly to Lewis. In Browning's case Lewis simply mistook a great strength for a weakness. On the other hand, Lewis's choice among his students as the most likely to get a first disappointed him by receiving only a third. Lewis's explanation of this fiasco was that his choice was a 'long distance runner who could not really be expected to show his excellence in a short race' (such as five consecutive days of written examinations!).

It took Lewis two full years to decide that one undergraduate in my class was probably incapable of passing the full honours course. It may be that Lewis was in a quandary as to what to do about the undergraduate concerned. He was certainly aware—he could not have failed to be—that something was wrong. But here again I have reason to believe that Lewis misinterpreted the evidence. I heard him say at a collection (while waiting my turn to have judgment passed) that 'Mr. Blank is guilty of certain sillinesses.' A year later Lewis abruptly presented the young man with an ultimatum: either take a pass degree (this was the degree without honours for the short two year course in English) or 'go down' (leave college) immediately without a degree. The unfortunate took the pass degree. Lewis might far better have forewarned the undergraduate at a very early date and so prepared him either for a supreme effort or quiet resignation. To my certain knowledge he did not take the trouble to do so.

To be sure, this case—like the relationship between tutor and undergraduate in general—was greatly complicated by the fact that most of the undergraduates immediately after the war were ex-servicemen, many of them having achieved high rank as wing commanders, colonels, or navy captains. It may well be that Lewis would have acted differently had he been dealing with a teen-aged schoolboy rather than with a hardened veteran in his mid or late twenties. But there is no doubt that Lewis's great fault, perhaps his only one as a teacher, was his basic lack of interest in his students as individuals. This is certainly borne out by his failure to cultivate in the least any of the undergraduates of the immediate postwar period, some of whom had had extraordinary war careers and had emerged from the experience as stimulating and worthwhile personalities.

Of course, Lewis was witty. I say 'of course' because wit is a cult at Oxford. No don could possibly afford not to be witty. Not brilliantly witty, be it understood. Brilliance is too close to the Oxonian taboo against parading knowledge, talent, or excellence in general. What is called for is dry, desultory, almost surreptitious humour, the nonchalant riposte, brilliance hooded like a falcon, or—and best of all—whimsy. The first person I met when I stepped into the Magdalen quadrangle was a former naval officer who accosted me with his address: 'Ah, you're Bailey, are you? Well, now that you're here, I suppose you're wondering what to do with yourself. Let me give you some advice. Get yourself a bit of supper, a jug of beer, go down to the river and punt off into the twilight.' In a sense I spent the next three years punting around in the twilight. But the point is that this was a prepared statement. God knows how long Dowrick, the former naval officer, had spent cooking it up. There are few things more elaborately contrived than the casual remark of an Oxonian. Oxford is the natural habitat of the intellectual ploy. A good portion of the undergraduate's—and the don's—time is spent in the preparation of rejoinders projected against occasions for their use. The occasions are inevitable because it is easy to ambush idiom. Sooner or later, for example, someone is bound to say something like: 'Fotheringay is a pretty good philosophy student, but he is a long way from Immanuel Kant.' The rejoinder: 'But surely the difference between the distance separating Fotheringay from Kant and the distance separating Fotheringay's tutor from Kant is negligible.' The complexity of the rejoinder is deliberate. By the time the other party figures out the import of the statement, it is just barely too late for a riposte.

Lewis himself was not above the deliberate ploy. He once ployed me during a tutorial, and then, when the opportunity again presented itself immediately thereafter, ployed his visitor—in my presence—with exactly the same words. But Lewis was credited with the best impromptu pun I can remember. The occasion was a dinner party. The main dish was a haggis, that fierce piece of Scotch culinary chauvinism consisting of the blood and guts of a sheep. Lewis was seated next to a Portuguese dignitary who, while partaking of the haggis, remarked that he felt like 'a gastronomic Columbus'. 'The comparison is wayward in your case,' remarked Lewis. 'Why not a vascular da Gama?'

In fact, Lewis was copiously endowed with native wit. He was in the habit of knocking out his pipe on the sill of the window overlooking the college gardens. On weekends these gardens are much frequented by out-of-town visitors. One Saturday afternoon after Lewis had just knocked out his pipe over the garden walk, a young man, an utter stranger, dashed into Lewis's rooms and shouted: 'Do you realize that you almost blinded my baby?' 'No,' said Lewis, 'I didn't even know you were married.'

Lewis was never one of the boys; he was naturally separated from the run of humanity by his fame, but he was careful to keep and cultivate the distance, and it was roughly the same distance as that separating Fotheringay from Kant. Just after the war J. A. W. (Jack) Bennett, then the Anglo-Saxon and language teacher at Magdalen, founded the Florio Club, a literary society open only to undergraduates reading English at Magdalen. We met once a month for a formal dinner, a speech by the guest of the evening (always a writer), and a discussion. There was never any question of Lewis's appearing at these functions in any capacity whatever. (The Florio Club also functioned as a sort of creative writing colloquium in which undergraduates would read their manuscripts aloud to the group for comment and discussion.) Lewis might easily have done so—some of the guest speakers were eminent men of letters, such as Joyce Cary. I remember that when John Betjeman was the guest speaker, Bennett poked some mild fun at Lewis, who, as it happened, appeared on the cover of *Time* magazine during that

week. In the same issue of *Time* there was a squib on
Betjeman buried in the literary section at the back
of the magazine. Lewis, of course, had been flood-
lighted by *Time* in his role as popularizer and apologist
for Christianity. As Bennett put it, there was 'a
much smaller but far more literary light' played on
Betjeman.

Lewis was not popular among his fellow dons. My
impression was that he kept almost as aloof from dons
as from undergraduates. As far as I know, he had only
two friends at the university, Professor Tolkien, and
Dyson, the English don at Merton. The lack of rapport
between Lewis and the dons at Magdalen, on their
side, was due not only to their envy of his fame but also
to their distaste of the nature of his fame and to their
suspicion of the achievement on which his international
repute rested. As popularizer of Christian dogma, Lewis
was embarrassing to the academic community. He once
complained of the lot of the Christian apologist:

> We who defend Christianity find ourselves con-
> stantly opposed not by the irreligion of our hearers
> but by their real religion. Speak about beauty, truth
> and goodness, or about a God who is simply the
> indwelling principle of these three . . . a great
> spiritual force . . . and you will command friendly
> interest. But the temperature drops as soon as you
> mention a God who had purposes and performs
> particular actions. . . . People become embarrassed
> or angry. Such a conception seems to them primitive
> and crude and even irreverent.[2]

I never heard Lewis or anyone else—including the college chaplain—discuss his religious works at Oxford. There was constant discussion, however, of Lewis's scholarly works, *The Allegory of Love* and *A Preface to Paradise Lost*. Both these books, and especially the former, are unquestionably among the finest examples of literary criticism in this century. These formed the basis of Lewis's towering reputation as a scholar. But, for the university, Lewis's standing as a scholar was checkmated by his unwelcome fame as an apologist of Christianity. The resulting ambivalence of his position virtually ruled out, I think, Lewis's ever receiving a professor's chair at Oxford. When the Poet C. Day Lewis (an outsider and the only other serious candidate) was elected Professor of Poetry by a wide margin, Lewis was cut to the quick. He publicly challenged C. Day Lewis to a contest in poetic composition with the chair as the prize. Shortly thereafter (1954) he was called to occupy the chair of Medieval and Renaissance English at Cambridge. He readily accepted. Oddly enough, the move also involved exchanging his fellowship at Magdalen College, Oxford, for a fellowship at Magdalene College, Cambridge.

The record—specifically the *Magdalen College Record* —shows that, apart from two years in the army during World War I and one year in London while he was trying his hand as poet, Lewis was always cloistered in the British tutorial system. I think it is clear that the grand passion of his life was reading. His description in *Surprised by Joy* of the keenness of his anticipation at the prospect of a weekend of undisturbed reading are the most moving passages in the book. He was certainly the most 'bookish' man I have ever met. He was not very good with people. This was not, it seems to me, because of some great inborn or acquired shyness. Lewis simply preferred books to people. I think his contact, his link, with humanity at large was the unbroken procession of undergraduates who were his pupils in tutorials. I think Lewis used his pupils as sounding boards, and, when they were superior, as debating partners for the forging of ideas in the heat of discussion. I count his lectures among the foremost of his intellectual products. Lewis was at his effective best as a lecturer. It was at the rostrum that he gave everything and took nothing—except the satisfaction of knowing that he was doing what he chose to do and doing it superbly. For it is here, I am convinced, that Lewis, the scholar, found his best fulfilment as a human being among his fellow men.

IN CONVERSATION

OWEN BARFIELD

Chapter Five

IN CONVERSATION

OWEN BARFIELD

The English, and still more the Scots, have the reputation of being a taciturn race. Yet reasonably fluent and relaxed conversation has undoubtedly played a large part in the development of their literature, at least between the days of the Mermaid Tavern and those of the coffeehouses of the eighteenth century. Indeed, it has often been observed that the best and most typical English prose style was born in those very coffeehouses. It is probable, however, that typical 'good' conversation among British literary men and artists does tend to differ in important respects from that of their counterparts in other races and nations. Coleridge's table talk was often characterized by those who heard it as 'brilliant', but it is very doubtful if the general conversation round the Gillman's table at Highgate would have qualified for that epithet.

What do people generally mean by brilliant conversation? It seems to imply a large ingredient of the sort of wit, spiced with malice, in which the circles round Madame de Sévigné, or round Voltaire, excelled. 'Brilliant', in fact, is taken in this context as almost a synonym for 'sophisticated'; and 'sophisticated' could perhaps best be defined as 'shallow without being clumsy'. While brilliance is entertaining and stimulating for short periods, it is rather tedious in large doses. Even the dull—perhaps least of all the dull—find this true.

At the opposite extreme from brilliance lies seriousness. Good serious conversation will be informed with wit, though less so than the brilliant variety, and the place of malice will be taken by a certain underlying solidity which is capable of degenerating into solemnity. Such we find in the recorded talk between the joint adherents of a French literary 'movement' like *symbolisme*. Perhaps a good start in distinguishing typically English conversation would be to compare *Conversations with Eckermann* on the one hand with Boswell's *Life of Johnson* on the other. Of course, this identification of cultural and social nuances with nationalities can itself be taken too seriously. There were other circles in eighteenth-century England besides Johnson's, and later on there was plenty of wit and would-be wit spiced with malice in Lytton Strachey's Bloomsbury. And so on.

Between these two extremes any conversation that was likely at any time to have taken place with or around C. S. Lewis was much nearer to the second than to the first. But it is a rather forced polarity. I could only achieve it by omitting another element that is especially characteristic of the best English conversation and which oddly enough seems to have begun to predominate at about the time of the Romantic Move-

ment and often in association with it. This is the comic
spirit or, if you will, humour. When Coleridge said to his
lifelong friend Charles Lamb: 'I think, Charles, you
never heard me preach a sermon?' and Lamb replied:
'My dear fellow, I never heard you do anything else!'
he was certainly being witty; but he was equally
certainly not being malicious. He *was* being comic. I
quote it, because it is just the sort of remark C. S. Lewis
might very well have made to a good friend, if he had
one like Coleridge. In fact, if one substitutes for 'My
dear fellow' something like 'On the contrary' or 'Good
heavens!' one can almost hear Lewis saying it.

Subject to an observation I shall be making later, no
one who has not spent many, many hours in conversation with Lewis can hope to form a proper notion of
what it was like, unless he is prepared, in his imagination of it, to accord a very predominant place to his
feeling for comedy. And this perhaps raises the general
question of the place of humour in human intercourse.
I remember once reading (I think it was in the early
days of Fascism) a casual allusion by d'Annunzio to
the 'destructive humour' of the English. If one recalls
the Malvolian solemnity of d'Annunzio and his admirers about his own rather limited gifts, and if one recon-
structs in imagination the probable conversation of
'd'Annunzio and his circle', there is matter enough for
comedy in that very remark. All the same there is a
grain of truth in it. In the parameter of conversation
between close friends, a sustained ebullition of humour
can perform two opposite functions. It can increase it
by enabling intimate allusions which would be crass or

indelicate in any other form. But it can also arrest the progress of intimacy at a critical juncture, whether it comes as the unplanned interruption by a ruling habit, or, used of set purpose, is raised like the traffic police-man's hand, gentler but not a whit less effective than the red light.

Some of those who have written about Lewis have emphasized his 'reserve'. It is true (though on reflection I have doubted whether it was as peculiar to him as such comments imply) that there were things one would have liked to talk of with him, but could not, because he would not. For casual acquaintances he had a peculiarly, perhaps deliberately, expressionless stare to show when the limit had been reached. For his friends he gave a comic turn to the whole conversation. As I cannot recall an actual example, I shall have to in-vent one. A. is talking with B. about, let us say, this very question of intimacy between friends. For convenience he applies to the problem of progressive self-revelation the metaphor of peeling an onion. B., however, sees what is coming and introduces into the conversation (but in a way that is very funny indeed) an allusion to another well-known characteristic of onions. Exit the intended topic, and a good time is had by all.

But if this negative aspect of humour must be taken into account in the matter of personal intimacy or familiarity, in the matter of intellectual intimacy and mutual understanding it is otherwise. Here there is no negative aspect and it is all gain. A good deal could be said about the absolute necessity of humour, as an available ingredient, to any really deep thinker, as distinct from either a merely rapid or a merely solemn one. But here I am concerned solely with its function in philosophical conversation. Here among the useful purposes humour can serve is one which can perhaps best be called 'packaging'. I am thinking more particularly of the kind of conversation Lewis describes in *Surprised by Joy* as 'an almost incessant disputation, sometimes by letter and sometimes face to face, which lasted for years'.[1] Packaging consists of tying up in a parcel and labelling for future reference a substantial stretch of the whole argument that has already taken place, not just its conclusion, but a lengthy process of discussion, comparing of notes, elaboration, disputation, followed by agreement or disagreement or half one and half the other. B. has endeavoured to establish a certain position—psychological, epistemological, philosophical, what you will. A.—or, since it is an actual example this time, let us say L.—has followed it with interest, but has criticized it at considerable length on the ground that it is too abstract and that B. is perhaps inclined to intoxicate himself with words. One or the other has thereupon suggested that trying to think it through is perhaps more like being snatched up in a balloon than going to heaven. B. has conceded that there may be something in this, has gone away and reflected further on it and has modified his position as a result of it, perhaps even modified somewhat his whole attitude to life or at all events to the relation between himself and life. This whole historical complex —something which, if it were a book instead of a conversation, would be, let us say, the whole of sections 2 and 3 of Part IV—is then mysteriously made available to both parties, for future reference and further development, under the name of 'Barfield's Balloon'.

When I am called on to speak or write about C. S. Lewis, it is usually not because I am regarded as an expert commentator in his many fields, but because it is known that I have a personal memory of him extending over a long tale of years. And I always find myself heavily stressing his irrepressible bent for comedy, simply because without that emphasis one would miss altogether the typical flavour of his company; and it is just that typical flavour that I conceive myself as expected to the best of my ability to supply. But I also realize that there is some danger of my being misunderstood. Lewis was not a social buffoon or a professional jester. I do not think I can recall his ever being flippant or merely trivial. Most often it was precisely because his fun was implicitly loaded with (perhaps rueful) experience or with tough thinking in the past that it was funny in the peculiar Lewis way. The almost habitual breeze of irony at his own, and of sarcasm at his friends' expense that rustled through it was never a bitter irony nor a biting sarcasm. It was much more like a 'language game', particularly so in the case of the sarcasm. There the object of the game was to come as near as possible to formulating an insult as if it were really intended, while at the same time choosing one which would be particularly telling if it were. He once carried this so far, or I was so stupid, that I thought it really *was* meant; and, for a time after that (but this was rather in correspondence than in conversation) we would preface with a solemn rubric to the effect that 'this is a joke'.

Aristotle advised his pupils 'paizein hopõs spoudazē' —to play in order to become generous or noble. This maxim incidentally is one I have more than once heard Lewis apply to the kind of taste for literature which he conceived it his job to strengthen and encourage in his pupils. But, when quoting it, he emphasized that 'paizein' really means 'paizein' and that therefore, while you are actually engaged in play, you must be minded *as if* the play were an end in itself. For otherwise you are not really *playing*, but only pretending to. He felt, I think, that the German idea of 'Humor,' for instance, is apt to overlook this condition and to be 'heavy', precisely because it can never manage not to remain faintly aware of itself as only a means to some higher end.

But it follows equally from the Aristotelian maxim that the play must not be of the mean kind that contradicts the *spoudazein* principle. Earnestness, when it was not explicit (and it was against Lewis's inclination and habit to make it explicit too often), was always implicit somehow in his context as a whole; and it was a mark of this that, although he would readily make fun of the great men of the past and exhibit them in a nonsensical light, he would only do so with those who knew and revered them as he did himself. A joke at the expense of Shelley or Goethe is a joke precisely *because* they were great men. In the mouth, or in the presence, of those who have never experienced that greatness, it is merely boorish. 'He's for a jig or a tale of bawdry!'

was a quotation often on his lips; and another was 'Let Gryll be Gryll and have his hoggish mind!' It would take too long, and would be too difficult, to illustrate properly the illuminating and enlivening use he made of quotation in general, for which he had a phenomenal memory. It was an element in which he and Charles Williams appeared to stimulate one another, and the best place to experience it was any meeting of the informal group known as the 'Inklings', which I was all too seldom able to attend.[2]

Another mark of his fundamental earnestness was his faculty of instant and close attention, not only to those who were in any way his match in learning or acuteness, but as much or more so on some ignorant or naïve mind with whom he happened at the moment to be in contact. Anyone who really *meant* something, however ill he expressed himself and however ignorant he might be of the fact that others had meant the same thing many times before, was sure of Lewis's careful attention and patient response. Partly he would play the Socratic midwife, putting more clearly what the other was trying to say, but partly also he would simply 'join in'. It could be quite a joy to listen in to such a conversation and hear him talking to his interlocutor. First he would speak as one simple man exchanging experiences with another, and only afterwards (if the occasion seemed to call for it and always without the least nuance of didacticism) would he bring to bear, out of his wide reading and phenomenal memory, some pithy utterance—it might be from Aristotle's *Ethics*, it might be from an Icelandic saga, it might be from George Macdonald—

that contained the very substance of what the two of them had just discovered they had in common.

His skill in dialectical obstetrics was greatly furthered by a characteristic, perhaps the only one, which he seems to have shared with Jeremy Bentham. And that is a certain delight in expounding the obvious and in expounding it meticulously and more than once. Whether this is a forte or a foible, it is something of which he himself was well aware. I recall one conversation with him, though the topic of it escapes me, in which at one point I had misunderstood him; and it subsequently transpired that I had done so because I had failed to realize that the proposition he was advancing with such precision, was one which we both, and most other men, took for granted. He himself suggested then that he was apt to spend time in verbalizing some truth so obvious that most people never think about it. And I suggested that others also did this, but that in his case the proposition was sometimes so obvious that other people were *not even conscious* of it! I mention this because I particularly remember his delighted laugh and his immediately adding that it was a very great compliment, as indeed, on reflection and by my own principles, it is.

It has been said that the ideal letter writer is the man whose letters sound as if he were still talking to you. If so, Lewis approached very nearly to the ideal; and it is fortunate that, even if I am not succeeding very well in evoking the qualities of his conversation, there are a large number of his letters extant. In many cases to read them is practically to hear him talking. This is true of a number of those in the volume *Letters of C. S. Lewis*, and many more will no doubt be made available when the authorized biography, now in the early stages of preparation, eventually appears. Meanwhile, if I now reproduce one brief letter in full, it may serve to illustrate alike the remark I have just made—the conversational tone of his correspondence—something of the nature of that conversation at its lightest, and the point made in the previous paragraph concerning his faculty of meticulous exposition and his own comic awareness of its occasional excess.

But I shall first have to explain the circumstances that gave rise to the letter. *Perelandra* had just appeared, and I had written him a letter in which I expressed my admiration for it and added one or two detailed comments. I think these were all laudatory, but in a subsequent letter, I took exception to the point in the narrative where Ransom, returned to Earth from Perelandra, is endeavouring to give his friends an idea of what that outlandish planet was like. 'Another way of putting it . . .' Ransom says, and we are given a second attempt to say in a different way what has already been said once. I complained that this held the reader up and was more appropriate to a lecture than a novel. Of course in this case it was very far from the obvious that was being expounded, and Lewis might well have drawn attention to this; he might also have pointed out that the passage was not directly narrative, but dramatic, and that the speaker within his novel was in fact a don with a don's mind and lecture-habit.

He preferred, as will be seen, not to defend himself.

He wrote me, in fact, in reply to the second letter, as follows:

> My dear Barfield—As all reviews of *Perelandra* so far have been unfavourable or non-committal you will imagine with what pleasure I read your letter at breakfast. Say what you like, there's nothing like a true friend. I am thinking of sending you a very judicious letter of general remarks on your qualities as a critic. . . . The devil of it is, you're largely right. Why can I never say anything *once*? 'Two and two make four. These pairs, in union, generate a quaternity, and the duplication of duplicates leaves us one short of five.' Well, all's one. Plague of these pickled herrings. I had decided before receiving your letter that the novel at present in progress is bosh. The same post brought a copy of the *Cambridge Review* which contained a letter pointing out a real howler in the Milton book. True friends everywhere; genuine amity is ubiquitous and affectionate veracity less uncommon than we suppose. And take that grin off your ugly face; remove that—hey! shut up. I'm getting I can't stop it.
>
> Yours
> C. S. L.

Since I have gone to the length of reproducing the letter, I suppose I had better footnote it (for this is also relevant to the purpose it is intended to serve here) to the extent of saying that the words 'very judicious letter' imported between us an allusion to the purported letter from a 'very judicious friend' which Coleridge included in Chapter XIII of his *Biographia Literaria*, and 'Take that grin etc.' an allusion (see *Surprised by Joy*) to the ways of bygone Wyvern Bloods.[3]

Lewis used to sit down and answer his letters, which became very numerous indeed, either before or immediately after breakfast. In this case it was clearly after; but the point is that he undoubtedly dashed off that one the moment after opening mine and certainly without pausing to reflect: how can I make this letter an amusing one? That was one of the differences between us of which I was always so well aware. It is just possible I might have put up a not less lively letter myself, perhaps even a not less apparently spontaneous one, but I should have had to ponder over it and take time selecting my amusing phrases—as indeed I sometimes did before I wrote to him—whereas *he* could be as pithy in talking as he was in writing. The rapidity with which his mind responded to whatever was presented to it, not only forming the necessary ideas but converting them simultaneously into well-ordered sentences, exceeded that of anyone I have ever conversed with. In later years especially, when I was also living a very different sort of life from his, I sometimes felt that he must be feeling I was dull, though there is fortunately some evidence that this was not the case.*
There are people in whose company I feel myself to be too quick-witted, so that I have to take some pains to avoid appearing aggressive; there are many others with

---

* In Chapter XIII of *Surprised by Joy*, Lewis identifies and lauds Barfield's major influence on his thinking. (Ed.)

whom I never think about it; Lewis was, I believe, the only person in whose company I frequently felt myself to be painfully slow-witted.

It follows from this that, when I suggested at the beginning of this chapter, that English conversation is typically humorous rather than witty, I had no intention of implying that Lewis was never witty, and witty in the ordinary, alert 'French' sense. He sometimes was and especially so when conversing with a group of talkers rather than with an individual. He was perhaps especially so when the group contained elements sufficiently antagonistic to his own tastes and convictions to prevent that undercurrent of personal sympathy out of which humour naturally flows. This was sometimes, of course, the case in the Halls and Common Rooms of Oxford, and the best example I know of a witty response from Lewis is recorded by Nevill Coghill in *Light on C. S. Lewis*. It occurred at Exeter College between Lewis and the Rector of the College, who was sitting next to him at dinner. I have Coghill's and the publisher's permission to transcribe it, and it went as follows:

'I saw in the papers this morning that there is some scientist-fellah in Vienna, called Voronoff—some name like that—who has invented a way of splicing the glands of young apes onto old gentlemen, thereby renewing their generative powers! Remarkable, isn't it?'

Lewis thought.

'I would say "unnatural".'

'Come, come! "Unnatural"! What do you mean, *'unnatural'*? Voronoff is a part of Nature, isn't he? What happens in Nature must surely be natural? Speaking as a philosopher, don't you know'—(Marett taught Philosophy)—'I can attach no meaning to your objection; I don't understand you!'

'I am sorry, Rector; but I think any philosopher from Aristotle to—say—Jeremy Bentham, would have understood me.'

'Oh, well, we've got beyond Bentham by now, I hope. If Aristotle or he had known about Voronoff, they might have changed their ideas. Think of the possibilities he opens up! You'll be an old man yourself, one day.'

'*I would rather be an old man than a young monkey.*'[4]

Lewis not only thought rapidly, but the clothing of his thought in words was equally swift. It was, however, remarkable in him that this rapidity of semantic utterance never gave rise to a corresponding rapidity of vocal utterance. That was always measured, always distinct. I never heard him gabble. Not only so, but I do not believe I ever heard him slur a single sentence. Whatever he was saying, and in whatever mood, his voice flowed evenly on. One could almost say it was the *kind* of voice one could hardly imagine doing anything else. I think most people found its timbre agreeable, perhaps partly because of the distinctness, but not only because of it. To try, however, to express in words the quality of a human voice is a hopeless task. Lewis himself used to remark how useless in a novel are the attempts of some writers to describe the faces of their characters, and it would be even more useless to attempt the description of a voice. It was low pitched. It was hollow rather than sharp. It seemed perhaps to issue from the whole of his head rather than merely from his throat. An enemy might even have characterized it as 'booming'. It was accompanied by very little movement of the facial muscles. Curiously enough, although radio was not a medium Lewis felt at home in, it was a voice that came over particularly well on the radio. I am not sure if he was ever televised, but there was a time, before the advent of television, when he was doing a good deal of broadcasting. I only heard one or two of the talks, but I was particularly struck by how unexpectedly well that voice recorded. It needed no tiresome artificial sprightliness to give it life. I also once or twice heard him take part in a broadcast dialogue, and again the medium seemed to suit him well. He could, I believe, have become a frequent and fairly popular broadcaster, if he had set out to do so.

But there was something in him that prevented it from happening, though I never quite knew what it was. It was not just broadcasting; it was speaking in public at all that he eventually took pains to avoid. I know this, because I happened to be in his rooms at Magdalen, Oxford, on an occasion not long before he left there for Cambridge, when someone rang him up evidently with an invitation to address an audience. He courteously declined it, but it soon became apparent that his caller was being importunate enough to press him for reasons. I heard Lewis reply that there were no particular reasons, but that he had recently come to the decision that talking in public, as distinct from writing, was not what he was cut out for; or words to that effect. I have no idea why this was so. I wondered at the time whether he had been disappointed at the reception accorded to him, but on reflection I doubt very much whether that was it. I got the impression that it was a theological or religious address he was being asked to give, and I dare say it was only from that particular field that he had decided to withdraw. But why? He had by that time preached a fair number of sermons, including at least one university sermon. Some of them have been printed, and I never heard or read an adverse comment on his delivery.

I never heard Lewis preach in St. Mary's, but I recall very well his doing so in London at one of a series of lunch hour services for city workers held in Southwark Cathedral. Given the difficulty inherent in what he had to say, its marked discrepancy, that is, from the journalist's idea of what constitutes popular Christianity, it seemed to me to be admirably adapted to his heterogeneous audience; and both his phrasing and his delivery retained as much of the sparkle of his private conversation as was compatible with the *milieu*. Yet he came to feel, as I have shown, that he had better give all this up. It remains a mystery, though it may well be that the solution is simple enough—the fear, for instance, of being drawn into stealing too much of his limited time from his true vocation of writing. On the other hand, there may have been some deeper reason, and it was this possibility, one he would prefer not to

discuss, that prevented me from questioning him about
it.

There is another thing that makes his virtual with-
drawal from public speaking rather puzzling. I have
described writing as his true vocation; and so it undoubtedly was. But we must not forget that he made his
living as a fellow and tutor, and later as a professor (he
gave away nearly the whole of his literary royalties),
and in that capacity had been delivering public lectures throughout the whole of his working life. My
experience of him in this role was again a very limited
one, and it is in any case dealt with elsewhere in this
volume. But I have one or two clear recollections which
perhaps I should recount. Very early in his academic
career I heard him give one of the lectures in his course
'Prolegomena to the Study of Medieval and Renaissance Literature' and I remember feeling that, however
excellent the subject matter, both the construction and
the delivery were rather lifeless. I even suggested to
him afterward, I think, that he might consider the ways
in which a good lecture differs from a good essay. I am
not under the delusion that he needed my advice, but
it is clear that he was learning his craft. To a considerable extent I should say he learned it on this very course,
which he repeated and developed over a long period.
What his later lectures were like may thus be gathered
from that scholarly, but deep and lively book, *The
Discarded Image*, published shortly after his death
which contains in a shortened form the substance of the
course.

My own most vivid memory of him as a lecturer,

however, takes me back to an afternoon in March, 1950, when I heard him give the Ethel M. Wood Lecture to a public audience under the auspices of the University of London, choosing as his title 'The Literary Impact of the Authorized Version'.[5] The hall was a large one and, unless my memory is at fault, the audience must have numbered not less than three thousand. Lewis spoke without notes or, if he had any, scarcely bothered to consult them. This time both his voice and his manner were full of life. He was genially in touch with his hearers, as he danced them along through his theme which was that there was virtually *no* direct literary impact at all.

I would give much to have heard those three Riddell Memorial Lectures (*The Abolition of Man*), which he gave at Durham University in 1943 and which contain much of his best and hardest hitting thought. I *did* hear, in 1942, 'Hamlet: The Prince or the Poem?'[6]—the Annual Shakespeare Lecture of the British Academy; but this was, by tradition I believe, a paper read rather than a lecture delivered. That makes it, excellent as it is, the less relevant to my topic here, which is C. S. Lewis as a talker; and I shall do better to conclude with some attempt at a general picture of his conversational powers. For all of us, as the years pass, reflective memory will be at its work of combining impressions that were faint and separate into some kind of significant whole. It can misrepresent and mislead as well as enlighten. It needs watching and checking. But I hope mine is not much at fault in presenting, as it has done, the combined effect of Lewis's substantial voice, the solemnity inherent in his large, inexpressive, curiously unlined face, and the abiding flow of his imperturbably analytical judgments as somewhat resembling a flood of clear and steady moonlight, settling downward from above and pouring tranquilly over the nooks and crannies of a conversational landscape.

ON THE AIR

CAROLYN KEEFE

Chapter Six

ON THE AIR

CAROLYN KEEFE

BROADCASTING TO BRITAIN

On August 6, 1941, as *The Times* of London ran the headline, 'Bombers Swoop on Sardinia',[1] C. S. Lewis spoke by radio to the British people. He did not mention air raids or invasions or war atrocities, yet indirectly he discussed these inhumanities and many more. His topic was 'Common Decency'.

Lewis talking over the British Broadcasting Corporation became a familiar sound. As far as I know, this early August broadcast was his first. During the next two years and eight months there were twenty-four more. To say that his voice was as well-known as Churchill's is an exaggeration; to repeat Warren Lewis's claim that his brother's name became a 'household word'[2] is closer to the truth. According to *Time*, an average audience of 600,000 heard each talk.[3] Countless more read them, printed first in three separate books and later combined in *Mere Christianity*.

Apparently some alert talent scout in the Religious Broadcasting Department of the BBC had predicted that Lewis as a convert to Christianity, a layman, and a writer of scintillating prose would have listener appeal. That prediction came true. By 1944 Henry James Forman of the *New York Times* implied that all England was eager to hear him,[4] and by 1944 *Commonweal*'s Anne Fremantle reported: 'Miss Dorothy Sayers, Father Ronald Knox, Miss Barbara Ward, and above all, Mr. C. S. Lewis, are definitely English religious radio stars.'[5]

The *Radio Times*, published every Thursday and sold for ninepence, lists the current fare offered by the BBC. During a typical week of broadcasting, the BBC airs every conceivable type of programme—news, weather, discussions, reports, interviews, travelogues, book reviews, foreign language lessons, quiz shows, lectures, drama, oral interpretation, sports, music (high, medium and low-brow), prayers, devotionals, and religious services—and recently an excerpt from C. S. Lewis's *Mere Christianity*.

What sort of communications system is this, we might ask, which provides such a variety of programmes and which continues to broadcast Lewis's voice a quarter century after the original discs were cut? The present British Broadcasting Corporation, an outgrowth of a 1923 company, was formed in 1927. It is a public corporation chartered by the Crown and licensed by the Postmaster General. Although the Government has powers relating to the conduct and the technical means of broadcasting, the Corporation is run by an autonomous Board of Governors. The independence of the Corporation from the Government and Parliament is accepted as fundamental to British broadcasting.

Revenues to support this commercial-free system come from the annual licence fees and the excise duty paid by the users of the sets.[6] Thus Parliament delegates authority to the Board which manages the Corporation for the listeners who finance the operation.

Currently there are four networks; at the time of the 'Broadcast Talks' there were only two. The Home Service carried three of the four series: 'Right and Wrong: A Clue to the Meaning of the Universe' (1941), 'What Christians Believe' (1942), and 'What Christians Believe about the Nature of God' (1944). Lewis's talks on 'Christian Behaviour' (1942) had a wider audience. Via the General Forces Programme not only the United Kingdom listeners but British servicemen all over the world heard him explain: 'Even while we kill and punish we must try to feel about the enemy as we feel about ourselves—to wish that he were not bad, to hope that he may, in this world or another, be cured: in fact, to wish his good. That is what is meant in the Bible by loving him: wishing his good, not feeling fond of him nor saying he's nice when he isn't.'[7]

C. S. Lewis speaking in this vein was not the BBC's innovative contribution to the war effort. From the very first days of the Corporation, religious programmes had been granted an important place and were planned according to three fundamental principles: 'The first is that the content of these broadcasts should be what is actually taught and practised by the principal organized expressions of the religious life of the country —the Christian Churches. The second is that these broadcasts should not be planned only for church-goers, but for all who wish to listen to them or view them. The third is that the standards of performance in religious broadcasting should be comparable to those demanded in other programmes.' [8]

In the Preface to the talks collection, Lewis shows his application of the first two principles. He explains that he was not trying to convert anyone to his own position but rather was attempting to expound and defend what he called 'mere Christianity' or 'belief that has been common to nearly all Christians at all times'. [9] He backs off from theological controversy by saying: 'I should have been out of my depth in such waters: more in need of help myself than able to help others,' and further-more, 'the discussion of these disputed points has no tendency at all to bring an outsider into the Christian fold.' [10]

Before Lewis delivered his second series in January and February of 1942, he sent the original scripts to four clergymen—an Anglican, a Methodist, a Presbyterian, and a Roman Catholic. He wanted to reach the greatest possible agreement on the topic, 'What Christians Believe'. According to Lewis, the differences which appeared were minimal: the Methodist objected that he had not said enough about faith, and the Roman Catholic contended that theories of the atonement were more important than Lewis had granted.

I do not know who Lewis's Anglican, Presbyterian, and Roman Catholic advisers were, but I am in touch with the Methodist clergyman, the Reverend Joseph Dowell who serves as Superintendent of the Darlington

Street Circuit, Wolverhampton, and Secretary of the Wolverhampton and Shrewsbury District of the Methodist Church. In a letter dated 30th January, 1969, Mr. Dowell recalls that Lewis sent the type-written radio scripts to him at Henlow in November of 1941. As Lewis says in the Preface, the Methodist made a suggestion about faith: give it greater emphasis. Dowell reports that Lewis did take his point. But on another matter, Lewis could not oblige. 'I did suggest that he should qualify his use of the term "good,"' writes Dowell, 'i.e. say whether he was using it in the sense of a "good thing" i.e. food for its purpose, or intrinsically "good in itself," or ethically—or as an "ultimate" good. In a letter which I unfortunately did not preserve, he mentions that he had to go, in the Broadcasts, like a "bull at a gate" and would have to avoid too much qualification.'

To his entire audience, Protestant, Roman Catholic, and nonsectarian, C. S. Lewis spoke about the merest beliefs that unite Christians. Using his almost exact wording but not the exact order of his ideas, I offer these points of summary from the radio talks: there is a Moral Law which we all know and all break; an evil power has made himself for the present the Prince of this World; man has free will; God is a Being who contains three Persons while remaining one Being; Jesus is the Son of God; Christ was killed for us, His death has washed out our sins, and by dying He disabled death itself; the Man in Christ rose again, not only the God; Christ's death somehow puts us right with God and gives us a fresh start; fallen man isn't simply an imperfect creature who needs improvement but is a rebel who must lay down his arms; a man is enabled to repent and pick himself up and begin over again after each stumble because the Christ life is inside him; Christians are Christ's body, the organism through which He works; God became man to turn creatures into sons, not simply to produce better men of the old kind but to produce a new kind of man; the new life is spread out not only by purely mental acts like belief but by bodily acts like baptism and Holy Communion; God is going to land in force in this enemy-occupied territory but Christians don't know when; and He is coming to judge the world at the end of time.

Not long after the speeches were aired, they were published in three slim volumes. The first appeared in 1942 under the title *Broadcast Talks: Reprinted with Some Alterations from Two Series of Broadcast Talks* ('*Right and Wrong; A Clue to the Meaning of the Universe*' and '*What Christians Believe*') *Given in 1941 and 1942*. The next year the text was printed here as *The Case for Christianity*. Then followed *Christian Behaviour: A Further Series of Broadcast Talks* and *Beyond Personality: The Christian Idea of God*. By 1945 C. S. Lewis was not only a radio star but a 'hot' literary property. His books were widely bought, reviewed, and discussed both here and abroad.

The book reviews are the best source for the answer to the question: 'How did the readers react to the "Broadcast Talks"?' They are numerous, accessible, and more useful than opinions expressed nearly three decades after the airing and the transcription. Reviews in Roman Catholic periodicals predominate. Out of the thirty-three reviews available to me, three are Protestant, ten secular, and twenty Roman Catholic.

Like most evaluations, these can be arranged on a continuum from enthusiastic approval to serious objections. With a single exception, the Protestant and secular reviews are complimentary. The twenty Roman Catholic reviews, while unanimously praising Lewis's style, express divergent opinions toward his handling of theology. From these I have selected three representative reactions to *Beyond Personality* or the 'What Christians Believe about the Nature of God' radio series. In *The Sign* Philip Ludden states categorically: 'A careful reading of his book . . . fails to reveal any explicit theological position which is objectionable from the Catholic angle.'[11] John F. Dwyer of *Thought*, published quarterly by Fordham University, takes a middle stance. He notes that even Lewis's best efforts have not enabled him to avoid a number of statements that seem to imply definitely Protestant, as against Catholic, viewpoints; however, Dwyer suggests that these points are of lesser stress and will attract the attention of only the theologian. 'The significant thing,' he recognizes, 'is that Mr. Lewis definitely allies himself with the foes of creedless Christianity.'[12] Thomas A. Fox is openly opposed to Lewis as a theologian. Admitting that the author has come a long way from his 'erstwhile atheism', Fox says that Lewis is still only growing up in the Faith. 'Inadequacy of doctrine, in whatever degree, is dangerous of course, and we should therefore place lay readers of Mr. Lewis on their guard.'[13]

These three examples show that some Roman Catholics did read the talks, write about them, and hold differing attitudes toward Lewis's theological approach. Inasmuch as I have not been able to obtain all the Catholic reviews of 'Broadcast Talks', I can only draw conclusions from the samples I did read. Out of twenty reviews taken from twelve different periodicals, only three raise strong theological objections, six note minor differences, seven stress agreement, and four fail to mention the subject. Although these numbers do not tell the whole story, they do seem to indicate that generally Roman Catholic reviewers do not think that theological differences, even where they exist, are serious and threatening.

It is quite evident, then, that C. S. Lewis had the ability to find the lowest common denominator of the Christian faith. But to broadcast effectively, Lewis also had to be attention-getting, clear, and interesting. A lacklustre introduction, dull material, muddled explanations, insincere approach, pompous or stupid attitudes, unprovocative analyses, poor diction, a harsh or monotonous voice—any one of these would have provided the listener with the excuse he needed to use his ultimate weapons: the dial change or the switch-off.

To my knowledge there is no dissenting opinion about Lewis's talent as a broadcaster. *Tablet* writer Robert Speaight reacts to Lewis-on-the-air: 'Mr. Lewis is that rare being—a born broadcaster; born to the manner as well as to the matter. He neither buttonholes you nor bombards you; there is no false intimacy and no false eloquence. He approaches you directly, as a rational person only to be persuaded by reason. He is confident and yet humble in his possession and pro-pagation of truth.'[14] Harold Gardiner of *America* calls him 'a superb teacher, not dry-as-dust, but friendly, patient, humorous and, above all, as any true teacher must be, deeply sensitive of the worth of those he is instructing'.[15] Another *Tablet* reviewers asserts: 'These talks are models of their kind, fresh and original in the illustrations used to clothe the basic arguments for accepting the Christian revelation.'[16] Katherine Tappert Willis of the *Library Journal* exclaims: 'How exciting he makes traditional Christianity.'[17] And so the reaction goes on and on, all laudatory, all indicating that Lewis had unusual skill in broadcasting. Even Alistair Cooke, the suave host of the former television show, 'Omnibus', credits Lewis with 'real radio talent'.[18] I say 'even', because Mr. Cooke is not a Lewis fan.

In the 24th April 1944 issue of *The New Republic*, Cooke makes a five-pronged attack against him: the war 'has pitch-forked Mr. Lewis into the limelight, for in doubting times completely unremarkable minor prophets are pressed into making a career of reassur-ance'; his approach to complex questions of morality is simplistic; his sexual morality is Puritanical; radio encourages acceptance of Lewis's teachings 'as the sort of redemption we have all been waiting for'; and the personal values of several million people stand in imminent danger of befuddlement.

Had Mr. Cooke waited for a few years he might not have jumped to the conclusion that Lewis's popularity was a wartime phenomenon. He wrongly assumed that because Lewis came to prominence during the war, the wartime need for reassurance was the direct cause of his popularity. If such had been the case, when the end of the war also ended the need for reassurance (using Cooke's assumption), then Lewis and his message would have faded into obscurity. The exact opposite was true.

In regard to the charge that Lewis dispensed reassurance, it is obvious that Mr. Cooke does not understand either Jesus' words or Lewis's. There is nothing particularly consoling about forgiving your enemies (especially during hostilities) or repenting of your sins or submitting to God's control. And Lewis certainly doesn't promise instant serenity: 'All I'm doing is to get people to face the facts. . . . And they're very terrifying facts. I wish it were possible, speaking in wartime, to say something more agreeable. But I've got to say what I think true.' Lewis agrees that in the long run Christianity brings unspeakable comfort but not until the believer has gone through an initial period of dismay.[19]

It is somewhat understandable that Cooke accuses Lewis of persuasive pseudo-simplicity. In the 'Christian Behaviour' series against which Cooke levels this charge, Lewis covers the subject of morality in eight ten-minute talks. Of course, he cannot possibly present a thorough, scholarly analysis of the topic, and he does not intend nor does he profess to do so. 'If you are allowed to talk for only ten minutes, pretty well everything else has to be sacrificed to brevity,' Lewis openly admits.[20]

After criticizing Lewis for his superficiality, Cooke himself gives but brief treatment to Lewis's attitude toward sex and marriage. He calls the view 'Puritan' and thereby associates it with the public image of grey-frocked saints walking back and forth to church reading prayer books and repressing their bodily desires.[21] Such a label is unfair to Lewis who does not disparage sex or any other sensory experience, only the perversions of God-given pleasures. The sexual impulse, Lewis explains, is not a vice in itself but can become one through misuse:

> The inventor of the human machine was telling us that its two halves, the male and the female, were made to be combined together in pairs, not simply on the sexual level, but totally combined. The montrosity of sexual intercourse outside marriage is that those who indulge in it are trying to isolate one kind of union (the sexual) from all the other kinds of union which were intended to go along with it and make up the total union. The Christian attitude doesn't mean that there is anything wrong about sexual pleasure, any more than about the pleasure of eating. It means that you mustn't isolate that pleasure and try to get it by itself, any more than you ought to try to get the pleasures of taste without swallowing and digesting, by chewing things and spitting them out again.[22]

These are hardly the words of a so-called 'Puritan'; in fact, any person deserving this misapplied label would cringe at Lewis's frank approach to the forbidden subject.

Cooke's assertion that radio encourages the acceptance of Lewis's explanations as a 'sort of redemption we have all been waiting for' is a provocative but unsupported statement. Nowhere in the literature have I found that listeners or readers did (or do) respond with a deep sigh of relief to any of Lewis's talks. Likewise his contention that the personal values of several million people stand in imminent danger of befuddlement is not backed by a single example. Surely between the fall of 1942 when 'Christian Behaviour' was delivered and the spring of 1944 when the critique was published, Cooke should have been able to find some specific cases of confusion.

In the absence of any concrete information about listener feedback to 'Christian Behaviour', there is no reason to accept Alistair Cooke's notions. If he personally finds that the exposition 'comes out with a patness that murders the issues it pretends to clarify', then that is his opinion as a reader and nothing more. As I read the thin volume of talks on Christian morality, I can't miss the main point: God does want a certain quality of life from the believer, and as soon as that person thinks he has achieved a measure of success, he is guilty of the worst sin—pride. Speaking for myself, I admit that this idea isn't a bit befuddled, and it certainly doesn't bring me any sort of welcome redemption. How the multitude of listeners reacted is another matter. I can't make any wild guesses about that.

As I have been discussing reviewers' reactions, I have

not been using them as examples of how the man-on-the-street responded to the radio talks. The writers are literary critics who may or may not have heard the actual broadcasts. Unfortunately the audience reaction sources available to me are extremely limited. Walter Hooper reports that Lewis did receive many letters from listeners, but these were tossed in the waste basket. There is one periodical, however, which does carry a 'Points from Letters' column, and I now want to look at that source. Since 1929 the BBC has been publishing a weekly journal named *The Listener*. Serving as an important adjunct of the Talks Department, it carries texts of the main talks, reviews of books and broadcasts, audience comments, and also advertising. From 24th February 1944 to 6th April 1944, the text of each 'Beyond Personality' talk was circulated two days after Lewis delivered it. Listener and reader response first appeared on 2nd March and continued until the last issue in April.

These letters are especially interesting for two reasons. First, the writers discussed ideas rather than delivery or style. Anyone who has given speech critiques knows that it is much easier to comment on manner, voice, diction, grammar, and word usage than it is to analyse and evaluate content and reasoning. These correspondents, however, made very few references to the more obvious features of the talks and then always in conjunction with the ideas. Having the texts available did enable the audience to read and criticize what had been said, and this, I suppose, is the strongest justification for publishing speeches in *The Listener*.

The second reason for interest is that most of the published reactions expressed disagreement with Lewis. In fact, a Mr. W. R. Childe from Leeds made such defamatory statements that Lewis issued a public rejoinder. After insisting that the moral teaching of Christ is the most important thing in Christianity, Childe linked Lewis with religious bigots: 'If I tell Mr. Lewis that "feeling the presence of God in flowers and music" *is* Eternal Life, he may prepare his faggots for the usual heresy hunt in which Christian dogmatists have in the past so often liberated their own suppressed intellects and passions.'[23] Lewis challenged his accuser to find any passage in his works which favours religious or anti-religious compulsion. For that discovery Lewis pledged five pounds to any not militantly anti-Christian charity named by Childe.[24] The next week Childe absolved Lewis from the charge of preparing literal faggots; he suggested that the effect of 'Mr. Lewis's propaganda' is to isolate Christianity in a theological vacuum; and he neglected to specify his favourite charity.[25] Meanwhile other letter writers battled verbally about such matters as man's awareness of the Trinity, the Church's theological superstructure, the manifestations of God's immanence, divine initiative in revelation, and the practical problems of forgiveness. Several people restated Lewis's ideas and argued for his position. To Childe went the last word as well as the first; he exited in controversy with a Mary Watkinson of Brigg.

Through the media of radio and the printed talks, C. S. Lewis enabled thousands to do what he said each person in our civilization should do: 'to come to terms with the claims of Jesus Christ upon his life'.[26] Lewis's talks begin in philosophy with the universal awareness of what we ought, yet fail to do, and they end in Christianity with an explanation of what it means to give up the self to Christ. In between the first instalment and the last, Lewis discusses why he believes Christianity is true and what Christian belief is.

During those twenty-five talks he established himself as a concise and controversial expounder of basic Christianity. To some he became a patron saint of apologetics, to others a slick hawker of religion. But after all the strong feelings about Lewis's 'Broadcast Talks' are sifted out and the complimentary and unfavourable epithets are set aside, there is general agreement that he is an able communicator. He can take oft-discussed religious subjects, ferret out the essential ideas, and explain his and opposing ideas in such a way that theological study becomes understandable and interesting. When on occasion Lewis is flippant, at least he is engaging. When he is cursory, he could, given more time, be thorough. When he is dogmatic, he nevertheless has a reasoned sureness. And all the while, no matter whether he charms or infuriates, he offers his listeners and readers compelling arguments to choose, as he did, the Christian option.

BROADCASTING TO AMERICA

In spite of his success as a broadcaster, Lewis did not enjoy the work. In a letter to his friend Dom Bede

Griffiths, he compared the dilemma he faced in preparing a radio script with that of a victim being forced to lie on a Procrustean bed: not unless he made the talks longer or shorter than fifteen minutes could he say something that Griffiths and his friends would pass.[27] Chad Walsh speculates that broadcasting must have imposed a painful discipline on Lewis. His conclusion is based on a comparison of the three 'Broadcast Talks' books with three others—*The Problem of Pain*, *Miracles*, and *The Abolition of Man*. The latter group, Walsh claims, contains a greater amount of original thought than the radio talks. In them 'he could assume a more leisurely frame of mind, and willingness to grapple with ideas that cannot be adequately presented in measured particles of radio time'.[28] Walsh reports that when the broadcast series were over, Lewis notified the BBC that he would not be available in the foreseeable future.

During 1957 the Episcopal Radio-TV Foundation, Inc. of Atlanta, Georgia, decided to approach Lewis about speaking over the American airwaves. The Executive Director, Mrs. Caroline Rakestraw, had no personal entrée to him, so she contacted Chad Walsh who asked Lewis to record a series of radio talks for the Foundation.

Lewis addressed his reply to the Right Reverend Henry I. Louttit, Bishop of South Florida and Chairman of the Foundation's Board of Trustees:

My dear Lord Bishop
  I think I can undertake what you suggest—tape-recording the talks here in England. I am not quite

clear how many of such 15-minute periods are included. Ten?

The subject I want to say something about in the
near future, in some form or other, is the four loves—
Storge, Philia, Eros, and Agape. This seems to bring
in nearly the whole of Christian ethics. Wd. this be
suitable for your purpose? Of course I shd. do it on
the 'popular' level—not (as the four words perhaps
suggest!) philologically.

I shall be glad to hear from you on further details.

Yours sincerely,

C. S. Lewis.[29]

In view of Lewis's attitude, it is surprising that he
agreed to resume broadcasting. Possibly his friendship
with Walsh was a deciding factor. He later did dedicate
The Four Loves to him. The idea for a book on this subject had already been germinating in his mind, and
undoubtedly he viewed the talks as the forerunner of a
larger, published version. Then too, the honorarium
may have enticed him. Recently married and the father
of two stepsons, he needed to supplement his university
income, so he later told Mrs. Rakestraw. And finally,
he probably considered a brief taping schedule less
objectionable than repeated interruptions to his work.
At any rate, C. S. Lewis did agree to once again lie
on a Procrustean bed.

The taping took place at Recorded Productions
(London) Ltd., Morris House, 1, Jermyn Street, on
19–20th August, 1958. The day before Lewis was
scheduled to speak, Mrs. Rakestraw visited the

enormous, well-equipped studio so she could discuss final arrangements with the engineer, Mr. J. R. Hale. She heard a faint, almost imperceptible hum. Hale tried to find its source, and when he was unable to do so, he called in consultants who likewise admitted their puzzlement. Finally someone hypothesized that the subway which ran beneath the studio might be a contributory cause. The head of the London Transport was summoned, and he traced the hum to a fan in the subway. When he learned that the studio was preparing to tape C. S. Lewis, he agreed to turn off the fan for two days.

On the first day of the taping sessions, Lewis arrived two hours late and offered no explanation for his tardiness. As he entered the studio, 'one could feel everything popping', recalls Caroline Rakestraw. He was dressed immaculately, not in his usual casualness which Walsh claims 'approaches but never quite reaches the point of carelessness'.[30] He carried a Homburg and twirled a cane.

During the recording sessions, Lewis was alone in the large studio while Hale and Rakestraw shared the control room. Looking down on Lewis they saw a stocky man of medium height with a ruddy face and balding head. He held a thick, handwritten sheaf of papers, legible only to him. The manuscript had marginal notes and deletions. As Lewis read he flipped through the pages, lifting a sentence from here, a paragraph from there. Yet he had such ease that he never bobbled or made mistakes. And Mr. J. R. Hale watching the remarkable handling of the manuscript and listening to the speech text became so engrossed that he let the tapes run out and the reels spin around.

What these two heard was C. S. Lewis's discussion of the four Greek words for love: 'storge' or affection, 'philia' or friendship, 'eros' or being in love, and 'agape' or divine love. He considered the origins, characteristics, perversions, and values of each of the three natural loves. He did not stress their rivalry to God as much as 'their failure without God to be completely, or to remain securely, the sorts of loves they professed to be'. These loves, Lewis wanted his audience to believe, are second things which when treated as first things 'let us down while legitimately attracting us'. He viewed storge, philia, and eros as 'demigods', 'substitutes', 'a kind of mirage' in need of conversion into agape. Lewis conceived of agape's world as one of 'unbounded giving and unshamed receiving, where all blessed creatures need and know they need nothing but God and are therefore set free to love one another disinterestedly'. The natural loves can enter this world only through the 'eternal element' common with the love great saints have felt for lepers and convicts and persecutors. 'For it only is Love Himself; it only is holy; it only is the Lord.'

This summary gives only a general idea of what Lewis said. Missing are the things that interest, provoke, amplify, inspire, enchant—the apt illustrations, the gentle humour, the earthy yet lofty style, the surprising word combinations, the balanced and rhythmic patterns, the smooth flow of ideas. Not unless one reads the scripts, or better yet listens to the tapes, can he know what captivated Hale. And only a direct observer could say, as did Mrs. Rakestraw: 'His personality filled the room.'

There were several problems connected with the taping. Lewis rattled the script, thus producing distracting noises on the tapes. When asked to manage the pages more carefully, he refused but did say that he would stop talking when he moved from page to page. There was also the audio effect of Lewis's heavy breathing. 'His intake of breath was like a bellows,' says Mrs. Rakestraw. Lewis offered a matter-of-fact explanation: 'I'm Irish, not English. Did you ever know an Irishman who didn't puff and blow?' In addition, Lewis had some trouble with his voice. At times it sounded hoarse and raspy. Therefore he was given an opportunity to rest his voice during the afternoon of the first day. By the next morning there was noticeable improvement. Another difficulty arose in regard to time limitations. As a British broadcaster, Lewis was not accustomed to making allowance for carefully-timed commercials. According to habit he filled up the entire period and sometimes even went beyond it.

After the job had been completed, the informality of luncheon provided a chance for small talk. Lewis showed Mrs. Rakestraw photographs of his dog, his recently-acquired wife, and his two stepsons. He spoke about his affection for his dog. But he was disinterested in conversation about current events and expressed open dislike for American journalism. 'The American church press is Victorian and the secular press is pornographic,' he opined. His table talk, like his writing, was full of metaphors.

Apparently Lewis's concern for the series ended with the taping of the last talk. Mrs. Rakestraw had told him that some portions of his frank treatment of sex would have to be edited out for the American radio audience. Refusing to be less than candid, Lewis had relegated the adaptation problem entirely to her and did not choose to hear the completed job. Even in the studio he had appeared to be bored by replays. Not even the printed copies of the talks, which were later sent to him by the Foundation, evoked any written opinion or response. This attitude is consistent with what his brother reports: 'It was rarely that, to me at any rate, he expressed any reaction on his published works; once a book was finished it was finished so far as he was concerned. He never subscribed to a Press Cutting Agency, or even read the press reviews of his books in the paper which he took.'[31]

Lewis received an honorarium for services rendered. He had been promised a fee, but the Foundation had not specified the amount, and Lewis had not asked.

In January, 1960, almost seventeen months after C. S. Lewis's voice had been recorded in London, it was first heard in this country over WSB of Atlanta. Since then 'The C. S. Lewis Program' has been broadcast on about 250 radio stations in all parts of the United States. The series are not now being offered to radio stations, although the Foundation honours the occasional requests it receives. Study groups are constantly using the tapes as the basis for discussion. And recently the Foundation produced a retail cassette album, 'C. S. Lewis: Four Talks on Love'.

Had Lewis read this account of his broadcasting, he might have been amazed (and possibly annoyed) that so much fuss was made over an activity he neither sought nor enjoyed. If this had been his response, I might have reminded him of Jesus' parable of The Two Sons. When asked by their father to serve in his vineyard, one son agreed and then never did it; the other refused but eventually carried out his father's command.

Lewis said that he had been a reluctant convert to Christianity. So were most of us. But Lewis had the honesty to admit it and then had the discipleship to do unpleasant tasks. Because he did, we can still listen to him and learn delightfully.

NOTES ON LEWIS'S VOICE

CAROLYN KEEFE

Chapter Seven

NOTES ON LEWIS'S VOICE

CAROLYN KEEFE

These observations, based on my analysis of 'The C. S. Lewis Programme' broadcast in America, deal with the four variables of voice: time, loudness, pitch, and quality.

The edited talks were placed on ten five-inch reels which each run for an average of fourteen minutes and thirty-three seconds. Don Elliot Heald, an Episcopalian layman and the station manager of WSB-TV in Atlanta, serves as the announcer for the series, and Dr. Edward McCrady, Vice-Chancellor of the University of the South, presents Lewis and summarizes and reviews the talks. The featured speaker has approximately 82·6% of the entire radio time, the introducer 10·8%, and the announcer 6·6%. It might seem that McCrady has an undue share, but the fleeting nature of radio necessitates the summaries and reviews. Heald's time is standard for announcers—a brief opening statement and a longer close which can be partially deleted to accommodate a commercial message. Even (as in this case) when time is donated by the station, advertising is a part of the quarter hour.

Total programme length is not the only time aspect. Time also includes the speaker's rate per minute, the length of pauses between words, and the duration of syllables. On the ten tapes Lewis speaks from 138–161 words per minute. His average rate is 149. In surveying different types of radio speakers, James Murray found that educational speakers had a rate of 167 words per minute.[1] According to this standard, Lewis's speaking is slow, an observation Barfield makes about his friend's conversation.

Certainly the most important aspect of rate is its effect on the hearers. Diehl, White, and Burk found that neither the comprehension nor the listeners' evaluation of the speaker's delivery is changed by altering pause time within the range of 126–172 words per minute.[2] Lewis's rate, falling between both extremes, warrants the label of 'acceptable'. At the slowest rate his talks do not drag, and even at the fastest, his articulation is clear and precise.

Lewis himself comments on the time element in his speaking. In a letter to Mr. John S. A. Ensor, Lewis explains:

The most noticeable feature of the so-called Oxford Accent is what phoneticians call diphthongization e.g. *Ka-ut* for *coat*. The slower you speak the more this is exaggerated (indeed v. slow speech will produce it in *any* accent). On the air I'm told to speak slowly—with the result you people deplore. But it isn't *my* fault.[3]

Lewis overstated his case. The result is clarity, not deplorable speech.

Radio broadcasting has several loudness factors which are not operative in the usual platform situation. First, the level is regulated by the engineer. He determines the distance and angle of microphone placement which produce the speaker's most effective voice quality. On the control board he is able to take care of ordinary changes in volume. Second, the broadcasting studio is designed to provide the most ideal conditions for sound production. The ceiling and walls are covered with an acoustical material which absorbs, reflects, and transmits various parts of a sound wave. In this room the distracting noises of a live audience and the outside world, such as shuffling, coughing, horn blasting, and wheel rumbling, are completely excluded. Third, the listener himself selects the level most satisfactory to him and the conditions of the room. Because of these three factors, the loudness of the voice is largely controlled by agents external to the speaker rather than by the speaker himself. His role is to obey the signals of the director, not to adjust to the demands of the room and feedback from the audience.

In regard to Lewis's volume, several observations seem important. Generally the sound was recorded on a uniform loudness level. The combined experience of Rakestraw, Hale, and Lewis, plus the excellence of the studio and the equipment, account for this. Another characteristics of the talks is that Lewis does not use abrupt changes in volume to achieve dramatic effects. He neither whispers nor shouts. Never does he display the vocal antics of the high-powered salesman, the fiery orator, or the impassioned evangelist, but he uses force and emphasis on a conversational level to intensify meanings and to sharpen contrasts.

Admittedly I am not a pitch expert, so to accurately determine Lewis's pitch, I solicited the aid of a man with many years of experience as a voice teacher. Fritz K. Krueger, Assistant Professor of Voice at West Chester State College School of Music, listened to several passages which I selected as examples of Lewis's total pitch range. By humming Mr. Krueger matched the speaker's lowest, habitual, and highest pitch. Then he located these levels on the piano. He placed the lowest pitch at G♯ in the second octave below middle C, the habitual at C below middle C, and the highest at the next F. Relying on his knowledge of music and his trained ear, Mr. Krueger labelled Lewis's voice as baritone. He also made a number of descriptive and evaluative statements which I shall mention later.

Perhaps the most outstanding characteristic of Lewis's voice is the resonance. It has a richness of sound, an expansiveness and dimension, the sort of balanced tone you can obtain by regulating the treble-bass dials on a stereophonic instrument. The resonance in combination with the baritone pitch gives an impression of masculinity and strength.

The hoarseness which had bothered Lewis in the studio is not evident. Either the taping had been discontinued on the first day before the condition could become acute, or otherwise the passages that sounded strained were excluded from the tapes. Throughout the entire series the voice quality is constant, although Mr. Krueger did notice that at times Lewis exerted greater effort to sustain his basic tone.

Lewis's deep breathing, however, is audible on the tapes, particularly at a loud level of reception. I want to emphasize that his voice itself is not breathy; the gasps come at the juncture of inhalation. Some are deeper, longer, and more distracting than others. At times his breath intake is normal.

The reason for this condition is difficult to determine. Lewis himself passed it off as a joke, blaming his Irish heritage. Warren Lewis, when questioned about the matter, seemed never to have noticed his brother's breathing for speech. None of the literature refers to it. Thus I can merely speculate about the physiological cause.

Dr. Ralph W. Mays, Director of Internal Medicine at The Germantown Dispensary and Hospital, Philadelphia, ventures a guarded opinion. Deep breathing of the type I have described is often symptomatic of heart disease. The large intake of air carrying oxygen to the bloodstream aids the functioning of an overworked heart. A person may have breathing difficulties for many years before a debilitating case of heart disease develops, explains Dr. Mays. Shortness of breath can also be caused by the numerous pulmonary afflictions, such as emphysema or bronchial asthma, but with these maladies, the exhalation as well as inhalation is affected. Of course, a positive diagnosis cannot be made *in absentia*, Dr. Mays hastens to emphasize.

Dr. Mays's educated guess was stated prior to his

learning that at least by October, 1961, C. S. Lewis did have heart trouble.[4] In a letter to Dom Bede Griffiths, Lewis admitted that his condition was serious:

> Prostate trouble, by the time it was diagnosed, had already damaged my kidneys, blood, and heart, so that I'm now in a vicious circle. They can't operate until my biochemistry gets right and it looks as if that can't get right until they operate. I am in some danger—not sentenced but on trial for my life.[5]

In spite of the breath problems, Lewis's voice has superior quality. To me it sounds pleasant but not saccharine, confident but not cocksure, rich but not ponderous.

To the listener the time, loudness, pitch, and quality of a voice are not discrete, for together they produce a general effect. If there then is to be any projection of meaning and mood during the almost two hours that Lewis speaks from the tapes, it must come through the totality of his voice. Obviously Lewis could not rely on facial expressions, gestures, stage sets, audience interaction, mood music, or even his script to carry his message. By carefully choosing and arranging his materials and words, Lewis had cast his basic ideas into written form. But the same Lewis style that fascinates the reader could fail to grip the hearer, for unless Lewis's voice captures the pathos, the humour, the irony, unless from the analogies, instances, and illustrations it evokes sensory images within the mind of the listener, even his most excellent script will remain nothing but a sheaf of splendid writing.

On the tapes Lewis *does* mediate between the page and his audience. He speaks in a slow, evenly pitched voice and creates a drowsy, familiar, or sorrowful mood. He ridicules by uttering some words very slowly in a feigned solemnity and then rattling off others in rapid precision. He provides brief but choice moments of humour by giving imaginary dialogues in more than his usual pitch shifts. He uses a sarcastic tone, a superior, a sinister, an ominous one. Sometimes he seems to stand back with detached amusement and watch the human responses to love. And all the while, Lewis speaks with sense, fluency, and exactness, his mind, eye, and tongue working in almost flawless co-ordination.

When I first began to analyse Lewis's voice, I thought that it was deficient in pitch change, and then as I continued to listen, I realized that this very factor actually works to his advantage. Through it, as I have just shown, Lewis creates a variety of moods. And furthermore, on the monotone level, he is very humorous. In imagination I can visualize the accompanying facial expression—the fixed stare about which Hooper writes—and I can hear the mirthful response from the audience. Even a listener, separated from Lewis's bodily presence, catches this fun and with Lewis can laugh at love's extremes and enjoy its charms.

My own estimate of Lewis's voice was later confirmed by Mr. Krueger. He too notes that Lewis makes effective use of a rather even pitch. Lewis, he points out, maintains a basic fundamental sound, a timbre which has many qualities. Krueger refers to Lewis's nuances, the slight colour that gives meaning to his words. These accents have all the pressure they need. 'There are two impressions dominant in my mind,' is Krueger's summary judgment. 'One of two things is true: here is a man who is so perfectly trained that he is in complete control, or otherwise he is so naturally able and so confident of his ability that nothing stops him.'

NOTES

Preface

[1] 'Don v. Devil', *Time*, 8th September, 1947, p. 65.

[2] *The Times* (London), 25th November, 1963, p. 14.

[3] See Carroll C. Arnold, Douglas Ehninger, and John C. Gerber (eds.), *The Speaker's Resource Book* (Chicago: Scott, Foresman and Company, 1966) and Wallace L. Anderson and Norman C. Stageberg (eds.), *Introductory Readings on Language* (rev. ed.; New York: Holt, Rinehart and Winston, 1966).

[4] George Bailey, 'My Oxford Tutor, C. S. Lewis', *The Reporter*, XXX (23rd April, 1964), 37–8+.

[5] Jocelyn Gibb (ed.), *Light on C. S. Lewis* (London: Geoffrey Bles, Ltd., 1965), pp. 117–60.

[6] Owen Barfield, 'C. S. Lewis', Address given at Wheaton College, Wheaton, Illinois, 16th October, 1964 (transcript obtained from Clyde S. Kilby, Department of English, Wheaton College).

Chapter One

[1] Letter from Nevill Coghill, 7th July, 1967 (in the files of the author).

[2] Letter from C. S. Lewis, 13th March, 1944 (in the Lewis Collection, Wheaton College).

[3] *Ibid.*

[4] Letter from C. S. Lewis, 28th April, 1944 (in the Lewis Collection, Wheaton College).

[5] Letter from C. S. Lewis, 31st March, 1944 (in the Lewis Collection, Wheaton College).

[6] Letter from John S. A. Ensor, 9th December, 1965 (in the Lewis Collection, Wheaton College).

[7] C. S. Lewis, *Surprised by Joy: the Shape of My Early Life* (London: Fontana Books, 1959), p. 10. Quoted by permission.

[8] *Ibid.*, p. 16. Quoted by permission.

[9] Letter from C. S. Lewis, undated but probably Autumn, 1914 (in the Lewis Collection, Wheaton College).

[10] Lewis, *Surprised by Joy*, p. 134. Quoted by permission.

[11] *Ibid.*, p. 226. Quoted by permission.

[12] C. S. Lewis, *That Hideous Strength* (London: The Bodley Head, 1945), p. 211. Quoted by permission.

[13] *Ibid.*, p. 362. Quoted by permission.

[14] C. S. Lewis, *The Abolition of Man* (London: William Collins & Sons, Ltd., 1943), p. 12. Quoted by permission.

[15] C. S. Lewis, *Miracles* (London: William Collins & Sons, Ltd. 1947), p. 30. Quoted by permission.

[16] Susanne Langer, *Philosophy in a New Key* (Cambridge, Massachusetts: Harvard University Press, 1951), p. 40. Quoted by permission.

[17] Lewis, *Surprised by Joy*, pp. 218–19. Quoted by permission.

[18] C. S. Lewis, 'Myth Became Fact', *World Dominion* (September–October, 1944), p. 269.

[19] C. S. Lewis, *They Asked for a Paper: Papers and Addresses* (London: Geoffrey Bles Ltd., 1962), p. 164.

[20] *Ibid.*, pp. 164–5. Quoted by permission.

[21] C. S. Lewis, 'The Poison of Subjectivism', *Religion in Life* (Summer, 1943), pp. 356–65.

[22] C. S. Lewis, *Mere Christianity: A Revised and Enlarged Edition, with a New Introduction, of the Three Books 'The Case for Christianity', 'Christian Behaviour', and 'Beyond Personality'* (London: Geoffrey Bles, Ltd., 1952), p. 38. Quoted by permission.

[23] Alfred North Whitehead, *The Function of Reason* (Princeton: Princeton University Press, 1959), p. 68. Quoted by permission.

[24] 'Find the Balance', *Time*, 26th August, 1957, p. 34. Quoted by permission of TIME, The Weekly Newsmagazine; Copyright Time, Inc., 1957.

[25] Lewis, *Miracles*, pp. 49–50. Quoted by permission.

[26] Lewis, *That Hideous Strength*, p. 440. Quoted by permission.

[27] II Corinthians 13:8, Phillips Translation. Quoted by permission.

[28] Lewis, *They Asked for a Paper*, p. 196. Quoted by permission.

[29] Gibb, *Light on C. S. Lewis*, p. 63.

[30] C. S. Lewis, *Poems*, ed. Walter Hooper (London: Geoffrey Bles Ltd., 1964), pp. 34–5.

[31] C. S. Lewis, 'Meditation in a Toolshed', *Coventry Evening Telegraph*, 17th July, 1945, p. 4. Quoted by permission.

[32] C. S. Lewis, 'Religion: Reality or Substitute?', *World Dominion* (September–October, 1941), pp. 277–81.

[33] C. S. Kilby, 'C. S. Lewis and His Critics', *Christianity Today*, III (8th December 1958), p. 13.

[34] Gibb, *Light on C. S. Lewis*, p. 55. Quoted by permission.

[35] *Answers to Questions on Christianity* (Hayes, Middlesex: Electric and Musical Industries Christian Fellowship, 1944), p. 9. Quoted by permission.

[36] C. S. Lewis, *The Silver Chair* (New York: The Macmillan Company, 1953), pp. 16–17. Quoted by permission.

Chapter Two

[1] C. S. Lewis, *Letters of C. S. Lewis*, ed. W. H. Lewis (London: William Collins & Sons, Ltd., 1966), p. 48. Quoted by permission.

[2] Bodleian Library, MS. Top. Oxon. d. 95/1, fo. 5.

[3] P. C. Bayley, 'The Martlets', *University College Record* (1949–50), p. 12.

[4] MS. Top. Oxon. d. 95/1, fo. 8.

[5] *Ibid.*, fo. 14.

[6] MS. Top. Oxon. d. 95/2, fo. 44.

[7] MS. Top. Oxon. d. 95/1, fos. 17–18.

[8] *Ibid.*, fo. 12.

[9] *Ibid.*, fo. 17.

[10] *Ibid.*, fo. 72.

[11] *Ibid.*, fo. 109.

[12] MS. Top. Oxon. d. 95/2, fo. 123.

[13] MS. Top. Oxon. d. 95/3, fos. 62–77.

[14] *Ibid.*, fo. 70.

[15] *Ibid.*, fo. 77.

[16] *Ibid.*, fos. 108–9.

[17] C. S. Lewis, *Selected Literary Essays*, ed. Walter Hooper (London: Cambridge University Press, 1969), pp. x–xii.

[18] MS. Top. Oxon. d. 95/3, fo. 163.

[19] *Lewis Papers: Memoirs of the Lewis Family 1850–1930*, Vol. VIII, 69–71). The *Lewis Papers* (which are not available to the public) consist of one set of eleven volumes of letters, diaries, and other family documents in typescript compiled by Major W. H. Lewis from the original manuscripts. Major Lewis has granted me permission to quote from them here.

20 C. S. Lewis, *An Experiment in Criticism* (London: Cambridge University Press, 1961), p. 28.

21 MS. Top. Oxon. d. 95/4, fo. 17.

22 *Lewis Papers*, Vol. VIII, p. 245.

23 C. S. Lewis, 'Notes on the Way', *Time and Tide*, XXVII (9th November 1946), 1070–71.

24 *Lewis Papers*, Vol. VIII, p. 260.

25 MS. Top. Oxon, d. 95/4, fo. 31.

26 *Ibid.*, fo. 131.

27 First published by Oxford University Press in 1939, but I am quoting from the Oxford Paperback edition (1965) which is more accessible.

28 Tillyard and Lewis, *The Personal Heresy*, pp. 11–12.

29 *Ibid.*, p. 20.

30 Lewis, *Surprised by Joy*, pp. 228–9.

31 MS. Top. Oxon. d. 95/5, fos. 19–20.

32 *Ibid.*, fo. 20.

33 *Ibid.*, fos. 99–100.

34 It is most accessible in Lewis's *Selected Literary Essays*.

35 This is found in the essay 'Modern Theology and Biblical Criticism' in Lewis's *Christian Reflections*, ed. Walter Hooper (London: Geoffrey Bles, Ltd., 1967), p. 159.

36 MS. Top. Oxon. d. 95/5, fo. 132.

37 It is found under the title 'Psycho-analysis and Literary Criticism' in *Selected Literary Essays*.

38 MS. Top. Oxon. d. 95/5, fos. 132–34.

39 Now reprinted in Lewis's *Of Other Worlds—Essays and Stories*, ed. Walter Hooper (New York: Harcourt, Brace & World, Inc., 1966).

40 MS. Top. Oxon. d. 95/1, fo. 20.

Chapter Three

1 Lewis, *Letters of C. S. Lewis*, p. 200. Quoted by permission.

2 See *Ibid.*, p. 167 and Lewis, *Of Other Worlds*, pp. 35–8.

3 Lewis, *Letters of C. S. Lewis*, p. 205.

4 C. S. Lewis (ed.), *Essays Presented to Charles Williams* (Grand Rapids, Michigan: William B. Eerdmans Publishing Company, 1966), p. XI. Quoted by permission.

5 Gibb, *Light on C. S. Lewis*, p. 25. Quoted by permission.

[6] Tillyard and Lewis, *The Personal Heresy*, p. 69. Quoted by permission.

[7] *Ibid.*, p. 145. Quoted by permission.

[8] C. S. Lewis [pseud. N. W. Clerk], *A Grief Observed* (London: Faber and Faber, Ltd., 1961), p. 54. Quoted by permission.

[9] Lewis, *Letters of C. S. Lewis*, p. 307. Quoted by permission.

[10] C. S. Lewis, *Beyond Personality: The Christian Idea of God* (London: Geoffrey Bles, Ltd., 1944), pp. 1 ff. This address appears as the opening chapter. Quoted by permission.

[11] Lewis, *Letters of C. S. Lewis*, p. 193. Quoted by permission.

[12] Lewis, *Surprised by Joy*, p. 234. Quoted by permission.

[13] *Ibid.* Quoted by permission.

[14] *Ibid.* Quoted by permission.

[15] For further information about some of the less desirable features of barrack-room life see T. E. Lawrence's autobiographical account of his life as an enlisted serviceman in *The Mint*.

[16] Lewis, *Letters of C. S. Lewis*, p. 19. Quoted by permission.

[17] Saint Augustine, *On Christian Doctrine*, trans. D. W. Robertson, Jr. (New York: The Liberal Arts Press, Inc., 1958), Bk. IV, XII. Quoted by permission of the Liberal Arts Press Division of The Bobbs-Merrill Company, Inc.

Chapter Four

[1] C. S. Lewis, *The Allegory of Love: A Study in Medieval Tradition* (London: Oxford University Press, 1959), pp. 60-1. Quoted by permission.

[2] Lewis, *Miracles*, p. 99. Quoted by permission.

Chapter Five

[1] Lewis, *Surprised by Joy*, p. 207. Quoted by permission.

[2] For a description of the 'Inklings', see *Letters of C. S. Lewis*, pp. 13-15.

[3] Lewis, *Surprised by Joy*, p. 94.

[4] Gibb, *Light on C. S. Lewis*, p. 61. Quoted by permission.

[5] Lewis, *They Asked for a Paper*, pp. 26-50.

[6] *Ibid.*, pp. 51-71.

Chapter Six

1 *The Times* (London), 6th August 1941, p. 4.

2 Lewis, *Letters of C. S. Lewis*, p. 19.

3 'Don v. Devil', *Time*, 8th September 1947, p. 65.

4 Henry James Forman, 'Common-Sense Humanist', review of *Christian Behaviour* in the *New York Times Book Review*, 23rd April 1944, p. 12.

5 Anne Fremantle, 'Beyond Personality', review of *Beyond Personality* in *Commonweal*, XXXXII (14th September 1945), 528. Quoted by permission.

6 Burton Paulu, *British Broadcasting: Radio and Television in the United Kingdom* (Minneapolis: University of Minnesota Press, 1956), p. 4. See also Burton Paulu, *British Broadcasting in Transition* (Minneapolis: University of Minnesota Press, 1961), pp. 7–29; *Report of the Committee on Broadcasting 1960* (London: Her Majesty's Stationery Office, 1960), pp. 114–20; and *BBC Handbook 1970* (London: British Broadcasting Corporation, Broadcasting House, 1970), pp. 246 ff.

7 C. S. Lewis, *Christian Behaviour* (London: Geoffrey Bles, Ltd., 1943), p. 43. Quoted by permission.

8 *BBC Handbook 1955* (London: British Broadcasting Corporation, Broadcasting House, 1955), p. 57. Quoted by permission.

9 Lewis, *Mere Christianity*, p. vi. Quoted by permission.

10 *Ibid.* Quoted by permission.

11 Philip Ludden, 'Beyond Personality', review of *Beyond Personality* in *Sign*, XXIV (July, 1945), 667. Quoted by permission.

12 John F. Dwyer, 'Beyond Personality', review of *Beyond Personality* in *Thought*, XX (September, 1945), 573. Quoted by permission.

13 Thomas A. Fox, 'C. S. Lewis as an Apologist', review of *Beyond Personality* in *The Homiletic and Pastoral Review*, XXXXVI (October, 1945), 77. Quoted by permission.

14 Robert Speaight, 'To Mixed Congregations', review of *Christian Behaviour* in *The Tablet*, CLXXXI (26th June 1943), 308. Quoted by permission.

15 Harold C. Gardiner, 'Fine Theological Pedagogy', review of *Beyond Personality* in *America*, LXXIII (26th May 1945), 158. Quoted by permission. © America Press, Inc., 106 West 56 Street, New York, N.Y. 10019. 1945.

[16] 'Clear Reasoning', review of *Broadcast Talks* in *The Tablet*, CLXXX (18th July 1942), 32. Quoted by permission.

[17] Katherine Tappert Willis, 'Beyond Personality: the Christian Idea of God', review of *Beyond Personality* in *Library Journal*, LXX (15th March 1945), 264.

[18] Alistair Cooke, 'Mr. Anthony at Oxford', review of *Christian Behaviour* and *Perelandra* in *The New Republic*, CX (24th April 1944), 579. Quoted by permission of The New Republic, © 1944, Harrison-Blaine of New Jersey, Inc.

[19] C. S. Lewis, *The Case for Christianity* (London: Geoffrey Bles, Ltd., 1942), pp. 27–8. Quoted by permission.

[20] Lewis, *Christian Behaviour*, p. 7. Quoted by permission.

[21] For a comprehensive treatment of the Puritan Period, see Perry Miller, *The New England Mind*, Vol. I; *The Seventeenth Century*; Vol. II: *From Colony to Province* (Boston: Beacon Press, 1961).

[22] Lewis, *Christian Behaviour*, pp. 30–1. Quoted by permission.

[23] W. R. Childe, 'Points from Letters', *The Listener*, XXXI (2nd March 1944), 245.

[24] C. S. Lewis, 'Points from Letters', *The Listener*, XXXI (9th March 1944), 273.

[25] W. R. Childe, 'Points from Letters', *The Listener*, XXXI (16th March 1944), 301.

[26] Sherwood E. Wirt, 'Heaven, Earth, and Outer Space' (Part Two of an interview with C. S. Lewis), *Decision*, October, 1963, p. 4. Quoted by permission.

[27] Lewis, *Letters of C. S. Lewis*, p. 198.

[28] Chad Walsh, *C. S. Lewis: Apostle to the Sceptics* (New York: The Macmillan Company, 1949), p. 31. Quoted by permission.

[29] Letter from C. S. Lewis, 5th January 1958 (in the files of the Foundation.)

[30] Walsh, p. 14. Quoted by permission.

[31] Letter from W. H. Lewis, 29th July 1967 (in the files of the author). Quoted by permission.

Chapter Seven

[1] James Murray, 'A Survey of Rates of Radio Speech', *Western Speech*, IX (March, 1945), 2–7.

[2] Charles F. Diehl, Richard C. White, and Kenneth W. Burk, 'Rate and Communication', *Speech Monographs*, XXVI (August,

1959), 229–32. See also Carole H. Ernest, 'Listening Comprehension as a Function of Type of Material and Rate of Presentation', *Speech Monographs*, XXXV, No. 2 (June, 1968), 154–8.

[3] Letter from C. S. Lewis, 13th March 1944 (in the Lewis Collection, Wheaton College).

[4] Lewis, *Letters of C. S. Lewis*, p. 300.

[5] *Ibid.*, pp. 301–2.

BIBLIOGRAPHY OF ORAL MATERIAL

The following books include material originally presented by Lewis in addresses, lectures, sermons, papers, talks, and dialogue:

Rehabilitations and Other Essays. London, New York, Toronto: Oxford University Press, 1939.

A Preface to 'Paradise Lost': Being the Ballard Matthews Lectures Delivered at University College, North Wales, 1941. Revised and Enlarged. London, New York, Toronto: Oxford University Press, 1942. Published in America as *A Preface to Paradise Lost.* New York: Oxford University Press, 1961.

Broadcast Talks: Reprinted with Some Alterations from Two Series of Broadcast Talks ('Right and Wrong: A Clue to the Meaning of the Universe' and 'What Christians Believe') Given in 1941 and 1942. London: Geoffrey Bles Ltd., 1942. Published in America as *The Case for Christianity.* New York: The Macmillan Company, 1943.

Christian Behaviour: A Further Series of Broadcast Talks. London: Geoffrey Bles Ltd., 1943. New York: The Macmillan Company, 1943.

The Abolition of Man, or, Reflections on Education with Special Reference to the Teaching of English in the Upper Forms of Schools. London, New York, Toronto: Oxford University Press, 1943. London: Geoffrey Bles Ltd., 1946. New York: The Macmillan Company, 1947.

Beyond Personality: The Christian Idea of God. London: Geoffrey Bles Ltd., 1944. New York: The Macmillan Company, 1945.

Transposition and Other Addresses. London: Geoffrey Bles Ltd., 1949. Published in America as *The Weight of Glory and Other Addresses.* New York: The Macmillan Company, 1949.

Mere Christianity: A Revised and Amplified Edition, with a New Introduction, of the Three Books 'Broadcast Talks', 'Christian Behaviour', and 'Beyond Personality', London: Geoffrey Bles Ltd., 1952.

Published in America as *Mere Christianity: A Revised and Enlarged Edition, with a New Introduction, of the Three Books:* 'The Case for Christianity', 'Christian Behaviour', and 'Beyond Personality'. New York: The Macmillian Company, 1952.

English Literature in the Sixteenth Century, excluding Drama. Vol. III: *The Oxford History of English Literature.* Oxford: Clarendon Press, 1954.

Studies in Words. London and New York: Cambridge University Press, 1960.

The Four Loves. London: Geoffrey Bles, Ltd., 1960. New York: Harcourt, Brace & World, Inc., 1960.

The World's Last Night and Other Essays. New York: Harcourt, Brace & World, Inc., 1960.

An Experiment in Criticism. London and New York: Cambridge University Press, 1961.

They Asked for a Paper: Papers and Addresses. London: Geoffrey Bles Ltd., 1962.

The Discarded Image: An Introduction to Medieval and Renaissance Literature. London and New York: Cambridge University Press, 1964.

Screwtape Proposes a Toast and Other Pieces. London: Fontana Books, 1965.

Of Other Worlds—Essays and Stories. Edited by Walter Hooper, London: Geoffrey Bles Ltd., 1966. New York: Harcourt, Brace & World, Inc., 1966.

Studies in Medieval and Renaissance Literature. Collected by Walter Hooper. London and New York: Cambridge University Press, 1966.

Christian Reflections. Edited by Walter Hooper. London: Geoffrey Bles Ltd., 1967. Grand Rapids, Michigan: William B. Eerdmans Publishing Company, 1967.

Spenser's Images of Life. Edited by Alistair Fowler. London and New York: Cambridge University Press, 1967.

Selected Literary Essays. Edited by Walter Hooper. London and New York: Cambridge University Press, 1969.

God in the Dock. Edited by Walter Hooper. Grand Rapids, Michigan. William B. Eerdmans Publishing Company, 1970.